Klopp

Klopp

My Liverpool Romance

Anthony Quinn

faber

First published in 2020
by Faber & Faber Limited
Bloomsbury House
74–77 Great Russell Street
London WC1B 3DA

Typeset by Paul Baillie-Lane
Printed and bound in the UK by CPI Group (UK) Ltd, Croydon CR0 4YY

A CIP record for this book
is available from the British Library

ISBN 978–0–571–36496–1

In memory of Peter Quinn (1930–2019),
my dad, who first took me to Anfield

I'm not that interested in sport, but I'm so glad Jürgen Klopp is in the world and not only because my husband is a Liverpool fan. In the age of Trump and Johnson he delights me as an example of what male leadership can look like: passionate, humorous, generous, kind, driven by humility and integrity and, above all, decency. My husband loads up clips from post-match interviews and match highlights for me to watch and without fail Klopp makes me laugh or my heart swell.

Lucy Kirkwood, playwright,
quoted in the *Observer*

Contents

Prologue

On Wednesday 11 December, the eve of the 2019 general election, the Freiburg Baroque Orchestra performed Handel's *Messiah* at the Barbican Concert Hall in London. It was a joy – and a relief – to be in a place where the dismal sound and fury of Brexit couldn't penetrate, if only for a couple of hours. When the soprano opened Part III with the air 'I Know That My Redeemer Liveth' I found myself transported in a daydream of reverential delight. I imagine others around me experienced something similar. What a lovely phrase it is – *I Know That My Redeemer Liveth* . . . But on this occasion it wasn't the Divine I was pondering. My thoughts were more earthbound, temporal, absorbed in the wonders being wrought by a certain German maestro. And I don't mean Handel.

I was still thinking of the previous night when Liverpool FC had beaten Red Bull Salzburg 2–0 and thus qualified for the knockout stages of the 2019–20 Champions League. A victory masterminded by their inimitable manager Jürgen Klopp. Is he My Redeemer? No. Is he the Messiah? He's not even a very naughty boy. Is he the remarkable life-force driving a football club whose glory days looked to be a thing of the past? Most definitely. And the gratifying aspect of this union between club and manager is that it felt destined. A match that was meant to be. There is literally no one else you can imagine doing the job that Jürgen Klopp has done at Liverpool.

And yet ten years ago I had never heard of him. Not many had. Now, in 2020, he is probably the most famous and admired football manager in the world. How did this happen? Not being a passionate devotee of the German Bundesliga I was slow to catch on to the rise of a young coach who had made a name for himself at Mainz 05 and was resuscitating the fortunes of sleeping giant Borussia Dortmund. I think it was in 2011 when I heard his name for the first time. Liverpool were enduring an unhappy period in the doldrums, traduced by the financial mismanagement of Hicks–Gillett and, on the pitch, stuck in reverse under Roy Hodgson, a good manager in the wrong job. Names of his potential successors were being bandied around, as names will be, including that of Kenny Dalglish. But an LFC friend, one of a handful among our Friday five-a-side game in Clerkenwell, told me 'they ought to look at Jürgen Klopp'. Who? He gave me a thumbnail sketch, which I promptly forgot, diverted by the false dawn of Dalglish's second term and then the brittle magnificence of Brendan Rodgers's tilt at the Premier League title in 2013–14.

Ah, that was the season that was. Liverpool playing football at 150mph, spearheaded by an attacking trident that tore apart opponents at will, top at Christmas, five points ahead in March, surfing on a wild surmise that *we're gonna win the league*. However many the opposition scored we would contrive to score one more. Until we couldn't. On 27 April 2014, following Chelsea's 2–0 win at Anfield, aka The Day They Parked the Bus, I noted mournfully in my diary:

> . . . Glad it was Gerrard's mistake – he's the easiest of all to forgive. If Kolo Touré had done it, for instance, I'd have cursed Rodgers ever after for selecting him.

Meanwhile, over in Germany, Dortmund were beginning to make a noise with back-to-back Bundesliga titles, the Double in 2012, a Champions League final in 2013. Klopp was now on the radar. Following Liverpool's sob-story implosion under Rodgers and the disastrous endgame of his final months in 2015 (Stoke beating us 6–1 in May was the low point)* rumours of a replacement were twanging on the grapevine. Carlo Ancelotti was mooted. But the name that kept echoing back was Klopp. He had already decided to quit Dortmund and take a year off. Klopp: it had a ring to it, like a famous stand. Klopp: would the prospect of Anfield lure him out of his sabbatical? Klopp! Klopp! Klopp! The hoofbeats of destiny were picking up speed, coming closer. Some fans were now so enamoured of the possibility that they petitioned Klopp's wife on Twitter.

* To make matters worse it was also Steven Gerrard's final game for LFC.

Rodgers, having overseen a 1–1 draw in the Merseyside derby on 4 October, was sacked the same day. By the end of that week Klopp had signed a three-year contract at Anfield and was doing a walkabout on the pitch. Let it be noted that he looked great – imposingly tall, relaxed, dressed in jeans, black shirt, black blazer, his hair neatly trimmed. The famous smile was shyly in evidence. Then he did his first press conference.

After the mutual adoration and moist-eyed emoting that characterised his relationship with the Dortmund fans, Klopp dialled it down for his Anfield inauguration. He presented himself at the microphone in a thoughtful, quietly spoken manner. He was fully aware of the significance of his appointment ('It's the biggest honour I can imagine to be here') yet he didn't want to bang the war drum too early. The power chords of 'Heavy Metal Football' were kept in check. He was there to 'try to help' a club that, while underperforming, could hardly be considered in trouble. He couched his programme for renewal as a double appeal to the players and to the fans. If someone wanted to help the club they had to change 'from doubter to believer'. That was his second great soundbite. His first seemed to come by accident, though knowing his love of preparation he may just have made it look that way. 'Does anyone in this room think that I can do wonders?' he asked, immediately insisting that he was just a guy from the Black Forest whose mother was proud and probably watching him now on TV. 'So I am a totally normal guy . . . I'm the normal one.' Bullseye. His self-deprecation not only got a laugh, it placed him in pertinent contrast to the kind of football manager who might proclaim himself, say, 'The Special One'. Arrogance would not be the Klopp way. The only 'special' thing in his eyes was the club he hoped to serve. He understood Liverpool. He understood us.

He then pulled another masterstroke. 'I hope to enjoy my work,' he said, earnestly, looking directly at his inquisitors. 'All the people told me so much about the British press. So it's up to you – to show me they are all liars.' Another big laugh. He had disarmed the press by teasing them, and they loved it. What wonderful nerve to include *them* in his project: I propose to you football that everyone can enjoy, players, fans, managers, and yes, even you, the nasty, snarky hounds of the back pages. When someone asked him about the Anfield pantheon – i.e. the weight of history – he deflected the question by observing that no Liverpool manager had ever taken up the post already believing himself to be a legend. That sort of esteem had to be earned. He repeated something he had once said at Dortmund: 'It's not so important what people think of you when you come in. It's much more important what people think when you leave.' Again the humility, the sense of perspective, resonates. The person blessed with true confidence has no need to swagger or to showboat; and his self-awareness allows him to understand others. You could build a career on it.

A wise man once said, 'People don't believe in ideas: they believe in people who believe in ideas.' This is what Klopp got so right in his introduction that day. Conducting himself in a humble, humorous way, he set out key ideas – turning doubters to believers, the necessity of keeping your feet on the ground ('normal one'), the honour of serving a storied institution – which with patience and togetherness he believed had a good chance of being fulfilled. What's more, in pursuing these goals (and here is a crucial Klopp component) they would have *fun*. In the clenched, high-stakes business of the Premier League fun is the element that often gets lost. Managers take on a haunted look pretty quickly nowadays. Who can stand that much scrutiny? Or that much abuse? Ole Gunnar Solskjær went from bright-eyed charmer to wizened touchline Gollum in a matter of months. It's understandable to a degree: their jobs are permanently on the line. But even the grim-faced pundits on TV – Keane, Souness, Mourinho – look like they're auditioning for the remake of *Judgment at Nuremberg*. Klopp knows you must take your work seriously but not yourself, and that is the surest way to have fun.

Five years on from his arrival you would have to say his reputation has never been higher. There have been setbacks along the way – three lost cup finals – but they shrank to a footnote in May 2019 when Liverpool lifted their sixth European Cup in Madrid. Two other trophies, the UEFA Super Cup and the FIFA Club World Cup, followed in the autumn. Halfway through the 2019–20 season Liverpool were a runaway train, unbeaten for a year in the Premier League and heading towards their first title in 30 years. They had achieved this with football of such fluency, invention and ruthlessness that even rivals doffed their caps to them. The only thing that could stop us now was a global catastrophe.

This book is not a biography of Jürgen Klopp. If you want a factual record of his life and career there are such books available. I don't intend to write a conventional account of him, because he is not a conventional football manager. I'm pretty sure he is not a conventional human being. Writing about someone you admire can be a way of trying to understand that person. I want to examine the things that set him apart from other football managers. His sense of humour. His boundless geniality. His off-the-cuff smartness. His ability to inspire and command. His obsessive tactical nous. His amazing set of teeth. We have come to realise what a lucky time it is to be a Liverpool fan. I imagine there was a similar feeling when Shankly began exerting his authority at Anfield in the early 1960s.

For years it was the impossible dream. I wondered if I would ever see another Liverpool title victory in my life-time. I was a doubter, now I'm a believer. Klopp has made Monkees of us all.

1. Don't Mention the War

Marooned on the straggling outskirts of Liverpool, Huyton was once a pretty backwater of parks and greens and churches. Its parish roots can be traced to Anglo-Saxon times. In the middle part of the 19th century merchants and shipping magnates retreating from the city began to build large houses and estates there. Its prosperity was sudden, and short-lived. Like many such places its green fields and meadows were swallowed up by the black jaws of industry. Quarrying and coalmining became pivotal to the local economy, and once the railway arrived the population multiplied. By the 1930s its village character was all but forgotten. During the war two internment camps were established there, one for 'enemy aliens', that is, Germans, Italians and Austrians already resident in Britain, and one for POWs.

After the war the reputation of Huyton began a long and agonised decline, though it also figured in the news as the parliamentary constituency of Harold Wilson during his two terms as prime minister (1964–70 and 1974–76). Other names brought it brief renown. The painter Christopher Wood (1901–30) was a native, hated the place and got out as quickly as he could. The actor Rex Harrison (1908–90) lived on Tarbock Road before he became a star of the English stage and screen. Hard to credit that the man who played the debonair Professor Henry Higgins in *My Fair Lady* and gave Audrey Hepburn's Eliza Doolittle elocution lessons might once have spoken with a Liverpool accent. If he ever did he soon dispensed with it. I wonder if in their heyday he chanced to overhear his fellow Scouser and namesake George Harrison, whose Wavertree vowels were the flattest of all The Beatles: 'Clurr with the furr hurr.' 'No, George,' Rex would reply in his crisp Higgins manner. 'Let's try that again: "*Clare* with the *fair hair*."'

A Huytonian of more recent vintage is the elusive and enigmatic Lee Mavers, frontman of the great lost band The La's. Their mega-hit 'There She Goes' still gets regular airplay, its jangling chords and harmonies instantly redolent of the floppy-haired 1990s. It's not my favourite of their songs. That would be 'Son of a Gun', which opened their first and only studio album, *The La's*, a record Mavers subsequently disowned. The song distils in a haunting and beautiful way what I've always imagined to be the character of outcast Liverpool:

> *If you want I'll sell you a life story*
> *'Bout a man who's at loggerheads with his past all*
> *the time*
> *He's alive and living in purgatory*
> *All he's doing is rooming in hotels*
> *And scooping up lots of wine*

Come back, Lee Mavers, wherever you are. What the town is most famous for producing is footballers. Peter Reid, of Everton and England, was a Huyton lad. So too Joey Barton and Leon Osman. Its most revered son, as far as LFC fans are concerned, is Steven Gerrard, for years the club's Most Valuable Player, captain, lodestar, and perhaps, in years to come, manager. You can Google a photograph of Ironside Road, the cul-de-sac where he grew up. I also checked it on a map. It's a ten-minute walk from Hurst Park Drive, on the other side of Huyton Lane.

Which is where I grew up, in the late 1960s. By then the suburban sprawl that took hold between the wars was going modernist, post-industrial, high-rise. The town planners – those bogeymen of the 1960s and '70s – had torn down its gracious Victorian housing (and anything else of beauty or value) to throw up big estates. A brave new world, or so they thought. Ours was a semi in the middle of the Drive, an unexceptional house in an unexceptional road, though possibly a bit more comfortable than the tower blocks into which people were fast being decanted. I remember my terror of the kids who lived in Hurst Park Close – 'The Closies' – not least because some of them rode around on dogs. When I mention this to friends nowadays they guffaw – *You're making it up!* Only I'm not. I saw kids mounted on large dogs, bareback. I don't recall thinking that my surroundings were bleak or ugly, because they were all I knew. We were close to greenery with the King George V Memorial Playing

Fields – 'Georgy Fields', as it was inevitably known – and there was a back garden where we played footie.

I think I was possibly an eccentric kid, though close up all kids seem pretty eccentric to me. Childhood for most is a weird and fearful state: I wouldn't recommend it to anyone. I certainly must have *looked* eccentric, spindle-legged, bespectacled, with one lens patched up after an operation to correct a squint. 'Gozzy', as the condition was known. As a five-year-old I also insisted on wearing – riddle me this – a kilt, bedecked with a mini-sporran. I have no idea why. I had no Scots ancestry, so far as I knew, and I had no other designs on skirts. Maybe I just liked the look. This was the same impulse that determined my earliest allegiance to a football club. Which wasn't Liverpool, by the way. The first team I ever loved was Celtic, and not because of Kenny Dalglish or Jimmy Johnstone or Bobby Lennox or the 'Lisbon Lions' of 1967. All that came later. What I instantly loved and coveted was their green-and-white hooped top, which I first saw on David Perez, a good-looking footballer in my older brother's year at our new primary school. Those green hoops were like the rich electric green of a snooker baize, or the velvety green of our first Subbuteo pitch. The red and black Umbro logo winked like a ruby on the white shorts. All I lacked was the olive-skinned sexiness of David Perez. And the footballing skills.

I guess I first wore that Celtic top in April 1971, a gift on my seventh birthday, by which point football more

or less ruled my life. In May, I made my First Holy
Communion on the Saturday Arsenal beat Liverpool 2–1
in the FA Cup final, which was also the first time I'd ever
seen a live match in colour – our aunties in Old Swan had
a colour telly years before we did. Charlie George lying
star-fished on the Wembley pitch after scoring the extra-
time winner. I recall a general despond in the room at the
time – my family were all LFC fans – but I didn't feel
it. I was a Celtic fan, see, and in any case my interest in
football was too indiscriminate, too all-consuming, to let
a single result get me down. I lived football, in a variety
of forms. If I wasn't kicking a ball at Calderstones Park
(we'd moved by then) I was drawing pictures of football
matches in a scarlet spiral-bound notebook, or poring over
Shoot! magazine and memorising football scores from all
four divisions. Why? Because I was a boy, and that's the
sort of uselessly pedantic thing boys do. This was a time
when I honestly believed that a professional football team
lived on a terrace next door to one other, each billeted in
a house the same number as their shirt – so on LFC Street
Chris Lawler would live at no. 2, Emlyn Hughes at no. 6,
Steve Heighway at no. 9, and so on. It came as a shock to
learn that most of them lived in Tudorbethan mansions
dotted around Formby.

Back then I assumed that every other city was like
Liverpool, where football and music and religion were
just the elements you breathed. Only later did I realise that Liverpool was not like every other city – was

not like *any* other city. Geographically out on a limb, on the edge of the North West, its back was turned to the rest of the country. That didn't matter when it was the booming port of high Victorian England, the second city of Empire through which most of the country's wealth filtered. Liverpool's ship was always coming in, until it wasn't. Containerisation did for the sea trade, the economic centre shifted from the north to the south, and the liners began sailing from Southampton. No city, with the possible exception of Jericho, had suffered such a dramatic collapse. Economically in tatters, it got a reputation as a 'difficult' inward-looking place. Crushed during the Thatcherite clampdown of the 1980s, it was further damaged by certain wildcat politicians and other wilful saboteurs. In a generation we had gone from Beatlemania to *Boys from the Blackstuff*.

Not all criticism of the place has been groundless. The keen sense of grievance can come over as whingeing – 'Self-Pity City', as one newspaper called it – though that might be a result of the catarrhal accent that makes every sentence sound like a complaint. Our assertion of Scouse pride can sound defensive and tiresome to outsiders. The warm-heartedness of the people might be more appreciated if they didn't keep on telling you how warm-hearted they are.

And yet Liverpool *did* suffer in ways that exceeded other parts of the country. During the Second World War its strategic importance in the Battle of the Atlantic was not lost on the Nazis. During the Blitz of May 1941 German planes dropped 870 tonnes of high explosives and 112,000 incendiaries on the city. Around 1,700 Liverpudlians died in the bombardment and 76,000 were made homeless. That was in a single week. From August 1940 to January 1942 raids killed around 4,000 people in Liverpool, Bootle and Wirral, injured 3,500 and destroyed 10,000 homes. Other cities took a grievous pounding, with catastrophic losses of life and livelihood, but in terms of the ratio of deaths to population only London was more heavily hit than Liverpool. I was born in 1964, nearly 20 years after the end of the war, but the scars of those bombings were an overwhelming presence. You saw wide forlorn spaces everywhere, prairies of rubble and cinder, derelict buildings with windows like sightless eyes. A lone pub or church surrounded by wasteland was a common sight. An absence that felt like a presence. Researching that time had such an effect on me that I wrote my first novel about it.

If you want further evidence take a look at *Morning in the Streets*, an extraordinary BBC television documentary of 1959 that examines a city pickled in a raw post-war gloom. The terraces and cobbled lanes bear a gaunt, stricken look, as if the raids had happened weeks rather than years ago. This being Liverpool you hear a spirit of defiance and stoical humour in the montage of voices, and there are recurrent images of children gaily at play on a street or schoolyard. But no one watching could fail to see that the life here was tough, and comfortless. The war is hardly mentioned –

it doesn't need to be, because what these people are living in is a bombsite necropolis.

And who was to blame? If you grew up in Britain during the 1960s and '70s you could not escape the fact that the Germans were the most hated people on the planet. If your local environs didn't remind you of their evil legacy then cinema and TV and comics ('For you, Tommy, the war is over') would set you straight. The first film I remember watching on the big screen was *Where Eagles Dare*. The first comedy I remember laughing at was *Dad's Army*, though its credit sequence featuring those swastika-tipped arrows snaking through France and taking aim from across the Channel always looked a bit sinister. *The World at War* and its plangent title theme invaded living rooms in 1973. Around the same time the BBC drama *Colditz* became another obsession, which led me in turn to read *They Have Their Exits*, memoir of Airey Neave, the first Briton to make a successful escape or 'home run' from the prison fortress.[*]

At school, among the books that got passed around a lot were Sven Hassel's pulp novels – among them *Wheels of Terror*, *Monte Cassino* and *Reign of Hell* – about a German tank battalion of criminals and misfits brutally fighting their way through Europe. According to his website the Hassel oeuvre has been translated into 25 languages and

[*] He later became an MP and chief confidant of Margaret Thatcher. He was the shadow home secretary when killed by an Irish Republican car bomb in 1979.

sold over 53 million copies. I wonder if Jürgen Klopp (born 1967) was one of Hassel's schoolboy readers. He would have been the right age. Indeed I wonder what the young Jürgen felt about his homeland and its descent into the abyss. How did they teach Hitler and the Holocaust in German classrooms during the 1970s? His parents, Norbert and Elisabeth, would have been children during the war. What did they tell him about it? The knowledge of what their elders did (or failed to do) between 1933 and 1945 is quite a burden for the next generation to carry.

In the 1990s one of comedian Harry Enfield's less celebrated characters was a blond, bespectacled German student named – but of course! – Jürgen. At large in London he battens on to random strangers and engages them in stilted small talk until he admits, abashed, that he's German. In one sketch he's at a bus stop querying the late running of the service when he suddenly blurts out to the commuter next to him: 'I feel I must apologise for the conduct of my nation in the war.' The commuter, startled, replies, 'You weren't even born then.' But Jürgen will not be appeased: 'As a German I share in the guilt of my fore-fathers. The crimes committed during those dark years are a stain on my nation's history and [*rising to hysteria*] you must NEVER, EVER let me forget this.'

For some reason I can imagine the other Jürgen roaring with laughter at this. Perhaps he thinks, like the rest of us born at a safe distance from the war, *There but for the grace of Gott go I* . . . The accident of timing has spared us.

If Klopp had been born 50 years earlier in 1917 he would have been, as a 22-year-old, prime fodder for the German war machine, maybe flying one of the Heinkels or Junkers that bombed British cities; or, better suited to his tactical know-how, commanding a Panzer division in occupied Europe; or, if he'd been very unlucky, fighting to the last man on the Eastern Front. Stuttgart, Klopp's birthplace, endured its own rain of hell, raided repeatedly by British and American bombers. The worst of it came on 12 September 1944 when the RAF dropped 184,000 bombs, levelling the city centre and killing nearly a thousand people.

History, it's said, is the verdict of the lucky on the unlucky. What does Klopp feel – what does any modern German feel – when the latest WW2 blockbuster comes round? Fine when the Nazis get it in the neck. But Anglo-American cinema still loves to celebrate our vanquishing of the German rank-and-file, most of whom were conscripted in the first place. Even among more civilised voices one hears an old-fashioned relish for 'sticking it to the Krauts'. In his review of *Saving Private Ryan* the *New Yorker* film critic Anthony Lane wrote: 'Despite Spielberg's avowed intent to darken and coarsen the formulas of the war film, old moviegoing habits die hard: I was practically standing on my seat and yelling at Tom Hanks to kill more Germans, and then, when he had finished killing Germans, to kill more Germans.' It could make a people defensive, or paranoid, to realise how loathed they have been.

When Klopp was born in June 1967, Bill Shankly was almost exactly halfway through his managerial career at LFC. I doubt if he, or anyone else connected to Anfield, ever envisaged the possibility that one day a German would be in charge of the club. Imagine the reaction to it on the Kop ('The Germans bombed our chippy, la'!'). Shankly had played for Preston North End at Grimsby on 2 September 1939, the day before war was declared. It was also the day he turned 26, approaching the prime of his footballing life. Born in Glenbuck on the edge of the Ayrshire coalfield, he was a miner before he became a footballer. As he says in his autobiography (*Shankly*, 1976) he could have gone back to the pits or else stayed in his job as a riveter, making Hampden bombers. Instead he joined the RAF, where he also boxed and played football. His chapter on the war hardly mentions the enemy, aside from a close shave when his station at Manchester was bombed. He rose to the rank of acting corporal but had no urge to go higher: 'Even so, I was possibly a better example to the men than some of the sergeants were. I gave more advice than the sergeants did, and without the bull.' He disliked seeing any recruit being picked on for the sake of it. He once stepped in to prevent a fellow corporal victimising a boy because of his faith. 'I stopped that man from being stupid.' I bet he did. It's the act of a football manager in waiting. There are moments in *Shankly* when you are inescapably reminded of the manager who would come some years after him: the zeal, the vision, the wit, the common sense, the passionate commitment to improving, inspiring, winning.

But that's ahead of us. Given the ready availability of foreign talent and the money sloshing around the English league it's surprising how slowly German players were recruited. Surprising, that is, unless you happen to believe there was a residual antipathy towards Germany dating back to the war: The Hunforgiven. As a kid the only Teutons I had any affection for were Paul Breitner ('Der Afro') – no footballer had ever looked cooler with his socks rolled to his ankles – and Günter Netzer, a killer-blond midfielder who I always thought of as the German Tony Currie.

In the Premier League era suspicion of the old enemy was slow to thaw. Jürgen Klinsmann, deplored for his diving during Italia '90, became a hugely popular presence at Spurs in the mid-1990s, but there wasn't a rush of his countrymen following him. Andy Möller helped to set back Anglo-German relations years with his celebration of the winning penalty in the Euro '96 semi against England – hands on hips, chest puffed out. The pose seemed to embody a cartoon of *Übermensch* arrogance. Or maybe we just hated his poodle-rock hair. Arsenal, a cosmopolitan club, signed their first German in 1997 (Alberto Mendez, of German-Spanish extraction). Robert Huth came to Chelsea in 2001. Man Utd, remarkably, didn't sign a single German until Bastian Schweinsteiger in 2015. Per capita the likes of France,

Spain and Denmark have supplied far more players to British football than Germany.

The exception to this rule, of course, is the sainted Bert Trautmann, who between 1949 and 1964 made 545 appearances for Manchester City. Trautmann had fought on the Eastern Front, apparently with great distinction, before being captured at the end of the war and transferred to a POW camp in Lancashire. Offered the chance of repatriation in 1948 he chose to stay in England, working on a farm and playing in goal for the local team, St Helens Town. When news got out that City, a First Division club, had signed him it sparked protests, including a demonstration of 20,000 people outside Maine Road. How could a Nazi ex-paratrooper be allowed to besmirch our national game? Trautmann's personal decency, not to mention his ace goalkeeping, soon won the crowd round. He entered legend when he sustained a broken neck while helping his team to victory in the 1956 FA Cup final (3–1 against Birmingham City). He is surely the only footballer ever to break his neck in a match *and play on*. The break wasn't discovered until an X-ray examination three days later. Trautmann will also remain the only player ever to be awarded both an FA Cup winner's medal and an Iron Cross.

Liverpool weren't exactly in a hurry to sign their first German. Roy Evans got the ball rolling when he brought Karl-Heinz Riedle to Anfield in the summer of 1997. Riedle, part of the West German team that won the World Cup in 1990, was a rangy striker who scored some good goals during his two years at LFC. But he was unfortunate in his timing, having arrived just as the teenage Michael Owen was breaking into the side. In the summer of 2000 Gérard Houllier signed two German internationals, both defenders, with mixed results. Christian Ziege lasted at Anfield for less than a year, his signing from Middlesbrough more newsworthy – LFC were fined £20,000 by the FA for making an illegal approach – than anything he did on the pitch. Markus Babbel proved to be a fine marauding right-back in the Liverpool tradition, and scored the opener in the 5–4 win over Alavés in the 2001 UEFA Cup final. He promised much, before his career was cruelly interrupted by the paralysing muscular condition Guillain-Barré syndrome.*

But there was a German from that time who won lasting respect at Anfield. Dietmar Hamann – Didi – was a holding midfielder signed from Newcastle in 1999, beanpole-straight, mild-looking, enviably cool in possession. He often partnered Steven Gerrard, who later said that Hamann's defensive work and tackling allowed him to play further upfield. His finest hour, as every Liverpool fan knows, came in a match he didn't even start. At half-time in the 2005 Champions League final Liverpool were on the verge of complete humiliation, 3–0 down to a rampant AC Milan and seemingly out for the count. Rafa Benítez had taken an uncharacteristic gamble with

---

* Of which Mel Brooks once commented, 'When they name a disease after two guys, it's got to be terrible.'

his inclusion of Harry Kewell in the starting line-up. It didn't pay off, and after 23 minutes the sadly unreliable Kewell limped out of the action. Vladimír Šmicer, his replacement, was game enough but hardly the sort to orchestrate a Liverpool fightback. For the second half Benítez made a tactical switch by bringing on Hamann, whose unflappable presence disrupted Milan's rhythm and enabled Gerrard and Xabi Alonso to get forward. It led to the 'six minutes of madness' that turned the game around. (Šmicer, I never doubted you, honest.) The stereotype of Germanic efficiency and self-possession that had so often spread despond among British football fans was at last a weapon we had on our side: Hamann for All Seasons.

There followed another hiatus in which no German player came through the door at Anfield. Amid a flurry of desperate-looking buys in the last phase of Rodgers's tenure – let's hear the one-hand clap for Mario Balotelli (£16 million) – Emre Can arrived from Bayer Leverkusen for £9.75 million. Initially he was played in a three-man defence before Klopp moved him to a holding midfield role in which he often excelled and scored goals, including a spectacular overhead kick against Watford that was Premier League goal of the 2016–17 season. Contractual negotiations overshadowed his last season – he wanted a move, and eventually got one, to Juventus – though before he left he played his last game in a red shirt as a sub in the Champions League final of 2018.

That night in Kiev also marked the last competitive match our other German, Loris Karius, would play for LFC, and here we must pause to make an admission: Klopp doesn't always get it right. Liverpool had had a goalkeeping problem ever since Pepe Reina's departure in 2013. Simon Mignolet looked decent enough in the early days but was eventually exposed as a liability. You may recall a home game against Sunderland in February 2016 when, winning 2–0, fans staged a walk-out protest on 77 minutes against ticket prices. Unfortunately Mignolet also decided to take early leave – of his goalkeeping duties – and failed to keep out a curling free-kick from Adam Johnson (who ought to have been in prison at the time, but that's another story). Jermain Defoe equalised in the 89th minute. At the time it felt like another soft Liverpool capitulation; deep down we knew that a reliable goalie was a basic requirement of any club with title ambitions.

Karius looked a good prospect when LFC signed him in May 2016. He had already played for the Manchester City under-18 and under-21 teams and had just been voted the second-best keeper in the Bundesliga after Manuel Neuer. Klopp may also have had a soft spot, given the club they were signing him from was Mainz 05: the old school. By October Klopp had named him the team's number 1, at which point Karius revealed his propensity to drop clangers. His uncertain keeping was scrutinised in another collapse, against Bournemouth – 3–1 up with 14 minutes to go, 4–3 down at full-time – and Klopp twisted again by replacing him with Mignolet. He continued to defend Karius after he was restored to the side, seeming to regard the errors he made as an aberration rather than an intrinsic flaw in his game. When the press pounced on his mistake in allowing Leroy Sané to score at the near post in a tense 4–3 victory over City at Anfield Klopp dismissed the criticism as 'a hair in the soup'. Huh? We shook our heads and trusted him to know best. In retrospect Klopp's loyalty was a rare blind spot in his managerial vision – he simply couldn't see the accident waiting to happen.

When it did happen it was to be calamitous, a career-defining, cup-conceding nightmare from which there was no waking. We were just getting over the loss of Salah – courtesy of Ramos's sneaky judo throw – when early in the second half Karius collected the ball and, without pausing to check, bowled it out. Benzema stuck out an opportunistic foot and deflected it agonisingly into the net. Has a sillier goal ever been scored in a Champions League game? The second howler you could almost see coming when Bale, having just scored a worldie, had a quick look up and from 35 yards out blasted a left-foot shot straight at Karius – who somehow managed to punch it behind him into the net. *Caramba!* I felt for him in that terrible moment of humiliation. I also wanted to throttle him. Klopp, loyal as ever, exonerated his distraught protégé by insisting that he was already suffering a concussion, having been elbowed by the demonic Ramos. This may have been true; doctors checking him later said so. But you felt a sneaking suspicion that Karius – who I now thought of as preKarius – would have cost us whether he'd had a bang on his head or not. The mistakes were always in him.

When Bill Shankly took charge of the club in December 1959 Liverpool were still in the old Second Division. His first game as manager was against Cardiff, and we lost 4–0. 'After only one match I knew that the team as a whole was not good enough,' he wrote. 'We needed strengthening through the middle – a goalkeeper and a centre half and somebody up front to create goals and score them.' The three components, the spine, of any great team. After nearly three years at Anfield Klopp had everything but the right goalkeeper. It was as though he couldn't bear to see his young German fail. But by now the penny had dropped, someone had made a decision, and two months after Kiev LFC bought Alisson Becker from Roma for a reassuringly huge fee. We rejoiced – a top keeper at last! – and didn't mention the fact that the last time Alisson had played at Anfield we put five past him in the Champions League semi. His performances in the 2018–19 season were sensational: 21 clean sheets in the Premier League and many vital saves[*] earned him the Golden Glove award. Not to mention the profound gratitude of fans who could barely remember what a safe pair of hands looked like. In the Champions League final

---

[*] His injury-time save against Milik in the Champions League win over Napoli was magnificent, and season-defining. 'If I knew Alisson was this good I would have paid double,' said Klopp.

against Spurs in Madrid I thought Alisson was our man of the match.

I wonder if someone had to persuade Klopp that Karius was the team's Achilles heel. He often talks of the brilliant people behind the scenes advising him. Perhaps he knows that greatness involves humility, and that admitting your mistake isn't a sign of weakness but of good sense. The LFC transfer policy, so often wrong-headed in the last 30 years, had got the final piece in place. A global outlook now holds sway at Anfield. In December 2019 fans were given an early present in Takumi Minamino, the first ever Japanese player to represent LFC. Japan – another Axis enemy of 75 years ago. Happy Christmas. War is over.

2. Lust for Life

Whenever I start to read a biography I brace myself for one major hump: the early years. It's not that childhood is uninteresting or insignificant. For some it can be absolutely formative. But I question the speculative account of the child offered as a blueprint to the adult, the idea of the unformed youth prefiguring the greatness of the artist/writer/politician/sportsperson/whatever. Greatness can spring from those who promised it least. When the biographer starts fossicking for clues in the ancestry, in the lives of the parents and grandparents, I feel my eyes glazing over. Most childhoods, barring war, traumatic illness or abuse, are quite unexceptional. Philip Larkin spoke for many when he called his childhood 'a forgotten boredom'. Cinema gets around this by the convenient device of the crackling 8mm film of the beach holiday or the birthday party that shows, in heartbreaking jerkiness, the parents capering and pointing their kids in the direction of the camera lens. The HBO TV hit *Succession* creates a Freudian mini-drama around its title montage of a patriarch and his young family, smartly turned-out for the home movie and then ignored, shunted to the side of dad's monstrous brooding ego. It's a sensational bit of dramatic shorthand (thrillingly scored on a brittle detuned piano, strings and drum machine by composer Nicholas

Britell) and provides in 80 seconds a picture of early life that a biography would toil over for pages.

Perhaps the real truth of childhood is that it passes without much notice. Children generally don't stare within their souls wondering what will become of them in the years ahead. They just get on with it, and in the getting on they acquire a little insight and they shed some illusions: in other words, they become somebody. There are exceptions, of course, to the biographical blank of childhood. Dickens – an exception at all times – endured a boyhood so awful he practically created grinding Victorian wretchedness in the public imagination. It wasn't just the fact of his being sent aged 12 to work at the infamous blacking-factory; thanks to his feckless parents he had already encountered fear, disgrace, bailiffs, debtors' prison, freezing empty rooms and a hand-to-mouth life of begging and borrowing. He never forgot it. *Oliver Twist, David Copperfield, Great Expectations* are the progeny of that unhappiness, and while one would not wish his terrible childhood on anyone it's unarguable that English literature would be much the poorer had he not suffered it.

Dickens had a long association with Liverpool, incidentally, both as a traveller (he sailed from the Pier Head to America, twice) and a writer. He often stayed at the Adelphi Hotel on his nationwide reading tours and sold out St George's Hall several times. Liverpool has always embraced a performer, and there was never a performer

like Dickens. On one visit in August 1858 an audience
of 2,300 people greeted him – the largest he had ever had
– and more than £200 was taken at the door. He wrote
exultantly to a friend of how he 'rolled on the ground of
my room knee-deep in checks'. The *Liverpool Daily Post*
described his reading as 'a miracle of dramatic art'. Had he
been alive today I imagine he would have loved taking the
stage at Anfield. That's Boz, la'!

My boyhood was free of Dickensian misery, thank God.
I was raised a Roman Catholic, and, unlike Dickens, was
close to my mother. She had no deep faith herself, and by
the end of her life (cancer, aged 62) she had more or less
lost it altogether. My father, on the other hand, was the
most quietly devout man I've ever known. For most of
his life he attended Mass every day, a rosary in his pocket.
His personal hero was the Italian saint Padre Pio, of the
famous stigmata. He wasn't a martinet about the faith
with his children – my two brothers and sister – but we
went to Mass on Sundays and were friendly with the
Redemptorist priests at our local church. My dad could
never persuade us, however, to join him on his monthly
visits to confession ('connies', as he called it). I have no
idea what he had to confess, by the way; his life was one
of almost selfless duty and forbearance.

I had a phase in my teens of being 'holy-moly', as a girlfriend of mine later styled it, and did a regulation stint as an
altar boy. If you ever heard a loud bong on the Communion

bell at Bishop Eton Church in the mid-1970s, that was me. But Catholicism didn't become a cornerstone as football did, or music, or drawing. This last was my earliest passion and went through stages of refinement, beginning with action pictures of football matches done in felt-tip (many, but not all of them, Celtic-based), later graduating to Ronald Searle's spindly Molesworth illustrations which I copied in exact detail with fine-nibbed Rotring pens, or 'technical drawing instruments' in the words of the company that made them.* My dad ran a stationery business, so we never lacked for paper. I had a small talent for copying, and that was it.

I don't know if my dad was fed up with me supporting Celtic, but he soon reset the course of my life when he took me to Anfield for the first time. April 1972. Roger Hunt's testimonial. The Liverpool team comprised every player from the 1965 FA Cup-winning side: Lawrence; Lawler; Byrne; Yeats; Smith; Stevenson; Strong; Peter Thompson; Callaghan; St John; Hunt. They played an All-Stars XI drawn mostly from the England World Cup team of '66. I have little memory of the game – Hunt scored a hat-trick – but I do recall the eye-popping green of the pitch and the heavy masculine stench of cigars and liniment. Dwarfed by the towering figures around me and deafened by the roar I tried to compete by shouting abuse at the ref and

---

* A German company, of course. So too are Staedtler and Faber-Castell, my other favourites. If investing in cars, sausages or pens, always trust the Germans.

felt mortified by the pipsqueak sound that issued from my mouth: I buttoned it thereafter. What excitement, though, and what a privilege to catch the end of that era, the last gasp of Shankly's first great Liverpool team.

My dad was a season-ticket holder from his youth. He went to Rome in 1977 for our first European Cup win, and to Wembley the following year for our second. In middle age he fell out of love with the game, I'm not sure why, and gave his season ticket to my older brother, Mike. I found it sad that in later years I couldn't talk to my dad about Liverpool, largely on account of his relentless negativity. 'What about that lot on Saturday?' he would say, grimly, even if we had won 5–0. He would conceive an inexplicable hatred of some player whom I would then feel obliged to defend, even if I didn't much care for him myself. In the end I found it easier to go light on the footie talk, or avoid it altogether.

It was as though once he'd secured my allegiance to LFC he couldn't bear to accept his own. But he did admit to liking 'the new feller'.

Jürgen Klopp's father, Norbert, was a born sportsman, tall and agile. He played in goal for his local club VfR Kirn, but not for the first team. Unable to make it as a professional he began an apprenticeship with a leather goods company and went on to be a salesman. It will not surprise Klopp-watchers to hear that he was charismatic, ambitious, demanding – a bit of a stickler. Having moved to Glatten in the Black Forest Norbert and his wife Elisabeth had two daughters before Jürgen was born in June 1967, the summer of love. Klopp Snr's love was decidedly of the tough sort. He made the son his personal coaching project, teaching him football, tennis and skiing. The instructor gave no quarter, putting his charge through a daily regime of sprinting and heading. If they played tennis Norbert strove to win every game. 'It was a far cry from being fun,' Klopp recalls. At school matches his father would patrol the touchline in a virtual frenzy. (What's bred in the bone . . .) That the son became a professional footballer was surely the fulfilment of the paternal programme. Klopp said, 'It was the first great fortune of my life to do exactly what my father wanted to do. I live the life he had dreamt about. Any other job for me would have caused friction.'

Schoolfriends remember the young Jürgen as easygoing, funny, not that conscientious but respectful of his teachers. He got his teenage kicks from 'football and girls' – hardly unusual – and rode about on an orange Vespa. His mother was (and still is) an even-tempered, affectionate and amiable parent: a good foil to the drill-sergeant dad. It was she who decided that the children should be raised Protestant, like her. Norbert, who died in 2000, was a Catholic. Perhaps it is the mixture of these two religious heritages that helped forge the son, the Protestant side being rational, orderly and hard-working, the Catholic devotional, romantic, partisan. In the Swabian Protestant tradition Klopp was taken to church by his grandmother, who would promptly fall asleep. The family prayed, but he regarded belief more as a form of common sense than a strict system. 'There must be something that leads us, that keeps us all in line,' he said in an interview with Sam Wallace of the *Daily Telegraph*. 'Being a Protestant is nice, it leaves a few doors open. It's obviously not that dogmatic.' He talks openly about his faith, though he is no missionary for it. When his father was away travelling all week his mother would sometimes chide her son for misbehaviour and ask, 'What if God sees you doing that?' He would reply, 'Ah, He won't worry about that, He's too busy.' So to Klopp's other gifts we might have to add that of mystic: he knows the mind of God.

That brings back an email exchange I once had with a writer friend. It was towards the end of the 2013–14 season, just after Crystanbul. City had beaten Villa to go two points clear at the top, leaving us in need of a miracle. I happened to mention to this friend, J, that I was praying for that very thing. From my diary:

> J: If I were God, and someone was praying to me for a FOOTBALL RESULT, I would make sure they got the opposite . . .
> Me: And that is why, despite your suspicions, you are not God.
> J: What a very Jesuitical reply.

I took that as a huge compliment. But I didn't get the miracle.

You wouldn't know it from his behaviour on the touch-line, but Klopp seems quite relaxed in his own skin. He has a calmness about him that may derive from the love of his mother, or from the love of God. Or from both. In a TV interview with Jana Schäfer he said, 'I am afraid of someone in my family getting ill. But I am not afraid of anything else in life. There is nothing so important to me that I could not bear to lose it. And that's why I find there is no reason to fear.' It is quite something to have reached your 50s and be able to say you are afraid of almost nothing. And yet there is no hint of braggadocio or even a challenge in his tone as he says it. 'The most important point is that this lust for life is actually concerned with my faith. I am a Christian and so I see life as a gift.'

That philosophy must have been a refuge when Klopp was hacking around lower-league football in the late 1980s. Being tall he was good in the air and had a useful turn of pace. He eventually caught the eye of Bundesliga second division side FSV Mainz 05, who signed him in 1990. Photographs of him during his early years there show a willowy-looking figure, possibly one better suited to tennis than football, with straw-coloured hair that droops in a boyish centre parting rather like Lee 'Kurtan' Mucklowe's in the BBC comedy *This Country*. On YouTube a sweet little film, *Jürgen Klopp – From 7 to 50 Years Old*, flips through the different ages like a family photo album: here is the cute blond kid (aged nine), the speccy teenager, the moustachioed 22-year-old looking like a Prussian cavalry officer, the mature footballer shouting at the referee or posing stony-faced, arms crossed for the camera.

In the early days he played in attack and midfield, later dropping back into defence. You can watch him score a header in a Bundesliga 2 promotion play-off in 1997 against Wolfsburg – and then make a dreadful error at right-back to gift the opposition a goal. Mainz lost 5–4. Klopp is fond of saying what an average sort of footballer he was: 'I stuck around like a bad smell. Saturday afternoon people would go to the stadium and Klopp would be there again. For eleven years they could watch me every weekend, whether they wanted to or not.' If, as Dirty Harry said, a man's got to know his limitations, Klopp knew his long before others did. But he was too thrilled to be playing professional football to dwell on his shortcomings. One teammate says, 'He didn't attempt to dribble, because he couldn't. He didn't look that quick over the first few metres but once he got going you could hardly keep up with him.' Others remember him shouting a lot and moaning at those teammates who he thought weren't pulling their weight or tracking back. The sort of player you might call a 'leader' on the pitch or, just as easily, a pain in the arse.

When Mainz were under the forward-thinking management of Wolfgang Frank the squad were introduced to a system of psychological training. Klopp remembers it as revolutionary. In one session the players had been asked to draw a tree: 'And there were all these little trees and my tree was as big as the fucking paper! But that was only because I couldn't draw. And the guy taking the session looked at it and said, "That's confidence!" Since then confidence has been my hobby.' I wonder if he used a Rotring pen.

A eureka moment. And yet confidence alone isn't enough. Confidence is a state of mind, whereas talent is a gift. You may often meet a confident writer, for example, who has very little talent. How else would vanity publishing thrive? David Bowie once said, 'The worst joke God can play is to make you an artist, but only a mediocre artist.' Most of us can do one or two things well, perform this or that to a bearable standard. But what if our deepest passion – for music, or drawing, or ballet, or acting – turns out to be something we're just not that great at? In sport one imagines it must happen all the time. We have read of the athlete or the player who starts out 'promising', seems to be going places, and then either because of bad luck or injury falls by the wayside. Or else because they found out their talent just didn't measure up.

Between 1990 and 2001 Klopp played 325 second division games for Mainz, a club record. Whatever he thought of his capabilities he was evidently good enough to hold down a regular place in the team. But it was mostly a struggle for survival, with no proper training facilities, a grotty changing room and a volatile atmosphere in the boardroom. During his 11 years as a player the club was managed by 14 different men. Peter Krawietz, who was chief scout there and is now his assistant manager at Liverpool, said that the constant pressure at Mainz had a lasting effect on Klopp. 'The house was on fire, all the time.' Nor was football at this stage his only preoccupation. Money was tight and he had a wife and child to support. He was also studying for a degree in sports science at Goethe University in Frankfurt. If the rough-house atmosphere at Mainz grounded him in team ethic, university life taught him the benefits of independent study and the value of problem-solving. He later said that being around educated people on a daily basis – the proximity of intelligence – may have saved him from failing as a coach.

The subject of Klopp's thesis may come as a surprise. Had I been asked to guess the title I might have ventured one that anticipated his personal vision, e.g. '*Gegenpressing*: Putting the Squeeze On in the Modern Game', or 'Brilliant Trees: Why Thinking Big is the Key to Confidence'. But no, his thesis goes under the earnest title 'Walking – Inventory and Evaluation Study of a Sport for All'. Walking! Of all the subjects he might have chosen. Not very sexy. Not very Klopp. But it got him his diploma in 1995.

Those years at Mainz, 1990–2001, are by coincidence the very same that bracket the golden era of another future manager. It was the period he played for the first team at Barcelona, where he helped them win their first European Cup in 1992 and six La Liga titles, four of them back to back (1991–94). His name: Pep Guardiola. The names of Klopp and Guardiola are entwined today as rival titans of modern football coaching. But as players they were a world apart. De Luxe to Economy. If they were TV cop shows Guardiola would be *Miami Vice*. Klopp would be *The Sweeney*. Or maybe you prefer the more proverbial model of the tortoise and the hare? Pep certainly got off to a flyer, playing for Barcelona youth before breaking into the first team, aged 20. Wiry and compact, with excellent close control and a range of passing, he was spotted by then manager Johan Cruyff as a future star. He established himself as a defensive midfielder in the Barça 'Dream Team' alongside the likes of Romário, Laudrup, Koeman and Stoichkov. On top of all the club silverware he won 47 caps for Spain.

The example of the elite footballer who becomes an elite coach is an ambiguous one. There seems to be no hard and fast rule about the transition. In the modern era Ferguson and Wenger are most often cited as models of the unfancied player who became a managerial giant. But then consider the names who made it both on the field and off: Cruyff, Beckenbauer, Capello, Ancelotti, Deschamps, Mancini. For homegrown examples you'd have to look first to Bobby Robson and Brian Clough, and then, of course, to Kenny Dalglish. Ripple-dissolve to 1985–86 when, having already won five league titles with LFC, he won the Double as player-manager *in his first season* – an achievement unmatched anywhere, ever, I'm guessing.

There is an argument that after an undistinguished playing career it might require an even greater strength of character to take on the job of coach. Fair enough, it wasn't Barcelona Klopp was taking charge of. The differences don't need to be pressed. But whether he made the grade as boss man or not, Guardiola could always point to his gilded record as a player and say, 'Beat that.' Out there on his first training session Klopp could only have said, 'I played for this club 325 times. And I have a diploma in sports science (with a thesis on walking).' He didn't even have his pro licence. But he *did* have a sound grasp of tactics from his time with Frank, and he also had the ear of Mainz chairman Christian Heidel. He was pitched into the whirlpool, player on the Sunday, manager on the Monday – sink or swim. His charges were a demoralised squad facing relegation with 12 matches to go. Initially Heidel and Mainz president Harald Strutz trusted him only as caretaker-manager. After two league wins he was appointed till the end of the season.

Perhaps it was that knowledge of his own inferiority as a player that made him more determined to succeed as a coach. Can humility and hard work co-exist with the headier forces of confidence and ambition? In the case of Klopp the answer was clear: they had to. Up till then his limit had been 'good enough'. Here was his chance to be better.

3. 'Who is in authority here?'

A passenger-cargo plane is flying across the Sahara. Inside, a small bunch of oil workers and off-duty soldiers are dozing, or reading, or listening nervously to the juddering engine of the run-down plane: are they quite safe in this two-bit tin crate? The cargo of barrels at the rear rumble precariously. In the cockpit the pilot looks grimly at his navigator, and points – outside, a huge sandstorm is brewing and heading right their way.

Cue the opening credits to *The Flight of the Phoenix*, not the terrible remake of 2004 starring Dennis Quaid but the brilliant 1965 original, directed by Robert Aldrich. You can feel what's coming. The pilot, Towns, played by a grizzled and ageing James Stewart, crash-lands the plane in the desert, miles from nowhere. There are casualties. Under the blazing sun the shaken survivors take stock. They have no radio and no prospect of rescue. There is food, but limited water. Walking during the day is impossible in the heat, and by night they're likely to get lost. What the hell are they going to do? Towns feels guilty about his piloting – he's experienced enough to have known better – though his navigator Lew (Richard Attenborough) is also to blame: he's a secret boozer who should have checked the engineer's report before take-off. And the men they're stuck with are an Anglo-American cast of unheroic misfits – Peter Finch,

Ernest Borgnine, Ian Bannen, George Kennedy, Ronald Fraser – incapable of much beyond pissing and moaning.

But wait, there is a loner among them who's a bit different. Heinrich Dorfmann (Hardy Krüger) is young, good-looking, studiously bespectacled, self-possessed. He intimidates the others, not just because he's German and standoffish but because he's smart. And he has a plan. He's an aircraft designer by trade, and he knows their only chance of survival is to build a plane from the wreckage of the old one and fly out of there. It's a nutso idea, but with no better one available they reluctantly start work on the 'Phoenix', the bird that is meant to rise from the ashes.

What makes this group-in-peril thriller soar (as it were) is the committed work of the cast – no actors ever looked so parched and blistered – and the superb screenplay by Lukas Heller.* When I first watched the film as a kid I was mostly horrified by the death and doom and seeming hopelessness of the men's plight. Watching it again as an adult I found much more to enjoy, specifically the antagonism between Dorfmann and Towns, a battle of wills between young and old, between technical innovation and benighted complacency, and surely the unspoken one between Germany and America. Two scenes stand out, the first when Towns, as self-appointed monitor, finds that someone has been stealing the water, now in

---

* By strange coincidence he was the father of the woman who once called me 'holy-moly' – talk about a link!

dangerously low supply. Stewart, with a mad-eyed accusatory sweep of the group, looks about fit to murder the man low enough to– 'It was me,' says Dorfmann calmly. 'And I didn't steal it. I took it.' A low mutter of outrage before he steps forward to explain: 'Whilst you people have been sleeping or pursuing your ridiculous interests, I have been working. And since I was working harder than you were I also needed more water than you did. However, it will not happen again. Because from now on we shall all work equally hard.'

For pure Teutonic nerve it's unbeatable, and instead of a pile-on the men go sullenly, silently back to work. Take it and like it. The wonderful thing about Hardy Krüger's performance here is that he never raises his voice. His leadership, his natural command, has simply cowed the others into obedience. But not Jimmy Stewart – not yet. He's still sore that this young pretender and his plan have made *him* look redundant. Lew, wavering between the German's imperious can-do and old-fashioned loyalty to his friend, privately defends Towns to Dorfmann: 'He was flying by the seat of his pants in planes that were nothing more than bits and pieces before you even went to school!' 'That's precisely what is wrong,' replies Dorfmann. 'He has remembered everything and learnt nothing.' Stewart's resentment boils on until a showdown becomes unavoidable. They stand in the midday sun at a distance from one another, like duellists. The others look on, fearful, fascinated:

Dorfmann: Mr. Towns. Who is in authority here?

Towns: (*A long, long pause – proud, but cornered*) . . . You are.

Dorfmann: Very well. Since I am in authority I have decided to finish this plane and make it fly.

And so we turn to Jürgen Klopp in 2001 about to take the controls at Mainz, not just to rescue them but to make them fly. We can imagine the doubters on hearing that the team's right-back is going to fill in as manager. Perhaps there were even players who wondered if 'Kloppo', who tended to shout at them for 90 minutes, was the best candidate for the job. To the press Klopp presented a front of self-assurance, claiming he had more faith in his abilities as a coach than he ever had as a player. Privately, however, he felt at sea, and later confessed, 'I couldn't even ask the questions at first because I had to pretend I knew everything already.' But he was shrewd enough to realise that he needed a right-hand man, a confidant, and he picked the best in Željko Buvač, his former Mainz teammate. The taciturn Serbian, nicknamed 'the Brain' by Klopp, was a fount of football knowledge, knew the Bundesliga inside out and had already gone into coaching. Indeed he might have got the Mainz job himself – he had the pro licence, for one thing. But Klopp, even without official qualifications, was the man of destiny, and he would describe his hiring of Buvač as the best transfer he ever made.

Klopp had learnt well from his master, Wolfgang Frank, and immediately reverted to the style of play he had pioneered during his two spells at Mainz. So out went the libero – the sweeper who brought the ball out of defence – and in came the back four. In training the players would run through obstacle courses to get the blood going. At sessions no one was allowed to stand still and wait. The principle of team effort became paramount, leaving no room for the fancy-dan individual – not that Mainz had one. Players were coached into pressing the space and closing down opponents that way: zonal marking as opposed to man marking. It demanded discipline and high levels of fitness, and with Klopp at the helm it became a reality. Having narrowly survived relegation in May the 2001–02 season saw them, incredibly, pushing for a promotion spot. Reporters from the national press began visiting the Bruchweg, their run-down stadium, and brought back colourful accounts of the loquacious new coach who was transforming the 'carnival club'. The donkeys all of a sudden looked a bit like thoroughbreds.

Klopp had built on the work started by Frank, but he wasn't slavish in following his principles. For one thing, Frank was a martinet who insisted on absolute adherence to his system. Klopp, by contrast, gave his players freedom to express themselves within the tactical framework. It helped that he was in charge of more technically gifted players than Frank had had at his disposal. By April 2002 they needed three points from three games to go up. They drew the first two 1–1, and went to FC Union Berlin on the last day needing only to avoid defeat. They arrived in the capital in an atmosphere of poisonous hostility. Not everyone was a fan of the plucky minnows, and Klopp's recent appearances on DSF, the Bundesliga 2 broadcasters, had earned him in some quarters a reputation as a 'smart-arse'. In his excellent biography of Klopp, *Bring the Noise*, Raphael Honigstein describes Union as playing 'with a knife between their teeth', surprising Mainz with their aggression. The score was 1–1 with eight minutes to go when Mainz conceded a goal. Frantically throwing everyone forward they conceded another. The team below Mainz had won, and the dream of promotion was gone.

In the dressing room Klopp wept *bittere Tranen* – bitter tears. Who wouldn't have cried in his shoes? To have come so near and to fall at the last was devastating. The team would have to be rebuilt. The stadium was already being rebuilt, at enormous cost, in anticipation of their promotion charge. Money was in short supply, again, but the good news was that Klopp had signed a two-year extension to his contract. He wanted to stay, claiming he didn't even have the 'right clothes' to manage another club. No one doubted that he was the man to banish the disappointment and make them go again.

But Job could not have endured what happened next. Mainz went again in 2002–03, hovering all season just below the promotion places before putting themselves in contention with a big 3–2 win over Eintracht Frankfurt.

Three games to go. Cue the intro to Queen's 'Under Pressure'. Hopes seemed to wilt after a 4–3 defeat at Ahlen, but they came back with a 5–1 victory over Lübeck. On the final day they faced Braunschweig away, needing to outscore third-placed Frankfurt by one goal to clinch promotion. They were 2–0 up in 20 minutes, then 4–0 up when Braunschweig scored a consolation goal in the last minute. At this point Mainz have the third spot and are heading for the Bundesliga. Meanwhile in Frankfurt the game isn't over, the home side is beating Reutlingen 4–3. Klopp and his players are listening in the centre-circle as the news comes in, praying for the final whistle. Eintracht go 5–3 up, with three minutes of injury time left. Surely not, not *again* . . . and with 30 seconds left another goes in. 6–3. Mainz are fourth, pipped for the second year running.

The horror, the horror. I find this almost unbearable, and I only had to read about it, years later.* How did Klopp stand it? On the night LFC beat Barcelona 4–0 he memorably referred to his players as 'mentality giants'. They had done the seemingly impossible in overhauling the mighty Catalans to reach the Champions League final. But how about his own triumph as a mentality giant? Back in 2003, with the wreckage of yet another promotion bid lying around him and the prospect of another

---

* You can relive the agony of that Eintracht game on YouTube. The sixth goal is just terrible, a soft header that the Reutlingen keeper feebly allows to bounce off his knee into the net. Reminiscent of the goalkeeping that used to plague Scottish football – only then it was funny.

hardscrabble season ahead, Klopp would have been for-given a certain weariness of spirit. When the team returned to Mainz the day after the Frankfurt debacle 8,000 people showed up in the town square to welcome them home. Seizing the moment, Klopp launched into an impassioned address in which he vowed they would pick themselves up and aim for the top once more. 'Anyone who writes us off is making a serious mistake,' he said. Mainz would rise again. The crowd cheered wildly. Managers offer fighting talk all the time: it's part of the job. But the manager who can offer fighting talk after missing promotion by a point one season and then by a goal the next must possess aston-ishing reserves of self-belief.

And so it came to pass. Having twice failed to clear the runway Klopp at last achieved take-off and piloted Mainz to the top tier. Ironically he did so in a season of deep mediocrity. They had lost their top goalscorer Andriy Voronin* to FC Köln. Results were indiffer-ent throughout the winter and at times Klopp himself seemed uncertain of how to stop the rot. At one point he organised a changing-room survey in which the players were invited, anonymously, to write down the reasons why the team was failing. This sounds like a desperate

---

* Yeah, him. A burly blond Ukrainian with a ponytail that lent him the look of a docker moonlighting as a porn star. He played like one too. Benítez signed him from Bayer Leverkusen in 2007 after being impressed by his performance against LFC in the Champions League, but the goals (six) came at a dribble. Ought never to have been awarded the sacred no. 10 shirt.

– and very un-Kloppish – thing to do. Who is in authority here? The survey proved a fizzle in the event; no one contributed anything of the smallest use. They would have to take on responsibility themselves, just like the great teams do. A flurry of late wins gave them a sniff of promotion, but as usual the decider would come down to the last Sunday. Mainz would go up so long as they beat Eintracht Trier at home and Alemannia Aachen, in third, failed to win at Karlsruher SC.

In the team dressing room Klopp put up a huge banner. It just read '*Jaaaaaa!*' Accentuate the positive. Eliminate the negative. Why the hell not? He had tried everything else. Mainz, praise be, got their win, 3–0, in front of a sell-out crowd. Like Groundhog Day, there followed an anxious wait in the stadium for the news from elsewhere. It arrived: Karlsruher had beaten Aachen 1–0. Mainz had done it at last. No team had gained promotion to the Bundesliga with fewer points (54) before. (They had also lost the fewest games – six from 34 – in the whole league.) Like they cared. Tiny, unfancied Mainz 05, 99 years after their founding, had hit the big time. One can imagine the bacchanalian scenes of joy in the town square the next day. Thirty thousand people came to salute the returning heroes. And stepping up to the mic was the man who had offered blood, sweat and tears for the cause. Only one word for it: Boom!

Interlude: Kudos from the Kaiser

The city of Mainz is also home to one of Germany's two public-service TV channels, ZDF. Raphael Honigstein recounts a period in Klopp's playing career when he pursued an interesting sideline – as a reporter. Having done a three-month stint on the regional sports desk of the commercial broadcaster SAT1 he was ready when ZDF were looking to recruit pundits for their coverage of the 2005 Confederations Cup, held in Germany as a prelude to the 2006 World Cup. As a local hero he fitted the bill, but did he have the chops to play an expert on national television? And would he make a good match with the channel's main draw, Franz Beckenbauer, the Kaiser himself? ZDF Sports editor Dieter Gruschwitz already knew that Klopp was articulate and witty, able to elucidate tactical nuances to an audience without talking down to them. He offered him the job of analyst. (Klopp: 'All I thought was, "I can watch World Cup games!"'.) World Champion Beckenbauer might have turned his nose up at sharing a screen with the Mainz coach, but he came round to the idea on discovering that Klopp was a natural – an entertainer as well as an expert. 'Beckenbauer's approval was like getting knighted for Klopp. If the Kaiser thought he knew his stuff, he really knew his stuff,' said Jan Doehling, the programme editor.

It was a learning process for him, all the same, faced with mastering the new touchscreen technology while broadcasting live from Berlin. Confidence wasn't a problem for Klopp, but just as with coaching he depended on the advice of experts to develop his talent. Indeed, listening and learning are part of the talent – only a fool thinks he can get by on inspiration alone. Gary Lineker wasn't always the suave old fox he is now on *Match of the Day*. Footage of his early years as the anchorman heir to Des Lynam remind you how awkward he used to be, hardly able to hold the screen without flinching, his flat Leicester tones an agony on the ear. Fortunately charm was his natural asset, and confidence would come later from absorbing lessons on how to project his voice and personality.

The ZDF coverage of the World Cup won TV awards in Germany, thanks in no small part to Klopp's charismatic performances. You can watch him on YouTube. Very blond with lavish sideburns, relaxed in T-shirt and jeans, he talks a blue streak in front of a live(ly) studio audience more redolent of a talent show. Which in a way it was. Klopp's talent for explaining the game made him a national star, and it also put him in the shop window as one of football's most astute young coaches.

Sorry, I left the story of *The Flight of the Phoenix* dangling. What follows isn't a plot spoiler, but it is a suspense spoiler, so if you haven't seen the film you may want to look away now. I recount it here because it might be one of the most brilliant and fiendish twists ever to grace a movie.

The stranded men have gone back to work on the plane, and an uneasy truce holds. Dorfmann is alone in the fuselage jotting down calculations when Towns and Lew enter and sit down next to him. (Poor Richard Attenborough's face by now looks like a charred turnip, pocked with painful blisters and nicks.) While they take a breather Towns idly picks up one of the German's magazines to flick through. It's the house mag of a model aircraft company. Towns is interested and says, 'This the outfit you work for? Didn't know they built the big stuff as well.' Well, replies Dorfmann proudly, the biggest craft we make is the Adler, a glider that has a two-metre wingspan. A beat. Two metres? Pilot and navigator look at one another uneasily. There must be a mistake ... Lew turns to Dorfmann: 'How much designing have you done on the, er, real thing?' 'Oh, no, you misunderstand,' Dorfmann replies. 'We make nothing but model aeroplanes. But the principles are the same.' He gets up and excuses himself – work to do.

A look of horrified disbelief has seized both Towns and Lew. How did they come this far without realising that the German only built the equivalent of Airfix models? 'He didn't even keep anything from us ...' says Lew, wonderingly. The black irony of it is suddenly, sickeningly apparent. Out there in the desert they've been constructing their own mirage. What will they tell the others? Lew, starting to laugh, notices Towns's grave expression and says, 'What's the matter – haven't you got any curiosity left? Wouldn't you like to know what it's like to fly in a toy aeroplane?' He continues to laugh, hysterically, until he gives way to sobbing.

Idea for a sketch

A small town in Germany. The past.

The scene: The boardroom of an amateur football club, a dilapidated, unglamorous place. The chairman and his managing director are seated at a table. Both wear the worried expressions of men involved in a relegation struggle. The chairman gets up and begins to pace the room.

Chairman: Seven points from safety. Three games left. How did we end up here?
MD: By losing all those games. And by you appointing four different coaches in a year.
Chairman: Do you think he can get us out of it?
MD: The kid? He's done all right so far. And it's not like anyone else wanted the job.
Chairman: Funny how he just emerged from nowhere.
MD: I like his confidence. Though how anyone understands the game plan is beyond me – his tactics board looks like something out of NASA.
Chairman: Let's hope he knows what he's doing—

Enter a gangly young man, bespectacled, blond, unshaven. He is wearing a Beatles T-shirt beneath his club hoodie. Under his arm he's carrying a sheaf of magazines, which he puts on the table alongside his bottle of mineral water. His toothy smile bespeaks an overwhelming geniality.

MD: JK! We were just talking about you. How's our escape plan?

JK: (Sits at the table) Purrfect.

Chairman: Have to admit, we're a bit anxious. Three games left . . .

JK: It is all cool. We are in a really good moment. The boys are ready to play for their lives, absolutely, and we will try to enjoy it. Yes, it's going to be difficult, no question, but that's football. I said to them, We've got nothing else to do, so we might as well give it our best.

MD: And they understand the tactics?

JK: One hundred per cent. (He unscrews the top of his water bottle and drinks.)

Chairman: Two wins and a draw . . .

JK: Is that what we require? I haven't looked at the table. I just make sure the boys are focused on each game as it comes. That's all we can do.

The managing director nods, appeased. He picks up one of JK's magazines and begins flicking through it.

MD: *Subbuteo Monthly*. You're a subscriber?

JK: For sure.

Chairman: I didn't know you played.

JK: Oh yeah. I coached two championship-winning sides, I think I told you.

MD: Ah. I thought you meant—

JK: There's a little photo retrospective of me lifting the Subbuteo League trophy. Page 23, I think.

MD: (Turning to page 23) Yes. Indeed. There you are.

He hands the magazine to the chairman, who looks bemused.

JK: Table football's Der Kaiser! Cool, yeah?

Chairman: So . . . when did you progress to the, er, real thing?

JK: (Smiling benignly) Oh no, you misunderstand. I've worked only in the Subbuteo League. Prior to now, that is.

MD: You mean you've never coached an actual football team before?

JK: (Shaking his head) But I think you'll find the principles are the same.

MD: I thought the principle of Subbuteo was 'flick to kick' . . . ?

JK: Ha ha ha! That is true. But the one I meant is to shoot the ball into the net. And make sure we do it at least one more time than our opponents do.

Chairman: (Distracted) Yes . . . that is . . . a useful principle.
JK: (Rising) Well, gentlemen, I'd better get down there.
   The boys are waiting.

He flashes another wide grin, scoops up his magazines and exits. A stunned pause as the two men consider what's just been revealed. Both have gone pale.

Chairman: He coaches Subbuteo teams . . .
MD: When he talked to us about 'thinking outside the box' I didn't realise the box he meant was cardboard and contained a green felt pitch. And toy goalposts.
Chairman: We're going down. We. Are. Going. Down.

His head sinks onto the desk and he begins sobbing quietly.

Curtain.

4. Made For Each Other

One day in November 1961 Brian Epstein and his personal assistant Alistair Taylor made their way down the steps of the Cavern Club on Mathew Street, Liverpool. The venue was a dank, sweaty, evil-smelling place, 'as black as a deep grave,' Epstein recalled. He'd rather have been almost anywhere else, but someone had tipped him off about the band due to play a lunchtime session there. He knew them a little already – they would hang around the family record shop he managed – but he'd never heard them play. Between songs the band smoked, ate, joked, drank, took requests. Their set was a little jaded, but Epstein thought 'something *tremendous* came over, and I was immediately struck by their music, their beat, and their sense of humour on stage . . . They were fresh and they were honest and they had what I thought was a sort of presence, and – this is a terrible, vague term – "star quality".'

The Beatles in turn were impressed and flattered by the attentions of the suave young entrepreneur. Within weeks they had agreed to let him manage them. Epstein wasted no time in organising a makeover – new suits, new haircuts – and drew up a contract that stipulated precisely how they were expected to behave: 'Onstage there must be no drinking, no smoking, no chewing gum, and especially no swearing. The audience is not there to talk to you so don't chat to the pretty girls while you're onstage. Be punctual. If you're scheduled to arrive at a certain time, make sure you arrive when you are meant to. Remember that you are professionals now, with a reputation to keep up.' Even John Lennon, the most recalcitrant and bolshie member of the group, kowtowed to these instructions. He later recalled that Brian 'made it all seem real. We were in a daydream 'til he came along.'

Alistair Taylor, the assistant, knew from the off that band and manager were made for each other: 'Just as Brian believed in The Beatles, it was clear from the very start that The Beatles believed in Brian.'

Hindsight tends to put a stamp of inevitability on historic encounters. We like to imagine meetings between the soon-to-be-famous as moments of destiny, as an alignment of the stars, whereas in reality things just happen that way. If Brian Epstein hadn't visited the Cavern that lunchtime and discovered The Beatles, someone else might have done – but we will never know. What's clear is that their connection was instinctive, and romantic,* as it would be for an entire generation to come.

---

* And maybe more than that in the case of Epstein and Lennon.
In the spring of 1963 the pair famously spent a lost holiday in Spain together, giving rise to rumours of a sexual liaison between them. Craig Brown examines the story in his recent Beatles book, *One Two Three Four*, though he doesn't mention Christopher Münch's quietly affecting feature *The Hours and Times* (1991), in which the holiday is the dramatic centrepiece. Ian Hart played Lennon as a mercurial tease, and would reprise the role three years later in Iain Softley's *Backbeat*.

'Liverpool was made for me and I was made for Liverpool,' said Bill Shankly, in one of his most lapidary pronouncements. Football is an after-dinner speaker's paradise of fateful meetings, signings, hirings, firings.* In the summer of 2008 a number of Bundesliga clubs were in search of a new manager, and, with a reputation burnished by his time at Mainz, Klopp was an attractive candidate. Initially in the chase were Bayern Munich, but they seemed doubtful as to whether Klopp would cut it as a Champions League manager. It would be interesting to know what put them off – the vociferous touchline presence, or else his lack of experience with big-name players? In the end Bayern did go for a charismatic fellow named Jürgen – but Klinsmann, not Klopp. Hamburg were also interested, but allegedly backed off after one of their delegation objected to Klopp's unkempt appearance and the fact that some of his players addressed him as 'Kloppo'. (I wonder how long that Hamburg talent-spotter stayed in his job?)

It left the door open to Borussia Dortmund (BVB), who pounced. Change at the Westfalenstadion had been a long time coming. The club had been underperforming for years, and had finished the 2007–08 season 13th in the table. Philipp Köster, editor-in-chief of *11Freunde* magazine, succinctly diagnosed the problem in April 2008: 'In the time it

---

* And non-firings: we will probably never hear the end of the story of how Alex Ferguson was one game away from being sacked in January 1990. It was an FA Cup tie away to Notts Forest, United sneaked a 1–0 win thanks to a Mark Robins header, and Fergie survived.

took for the ball to be won by the Dortmund defence and moved upfield to the strikers, some of the fans in the south stand managed to go and buy a beer. Twice. Dortmund can carry on like this. Or someone can ask themselves how they can get this team playing.' Someone eventually did. Hans-Joachim Watzke and Michael Zorc, chairman and sporting director respectively of BVB, were convinced that the man who would turn the club around was Jürgen Klopp. So what if he was inexperienced? He was also a breath of fresh air, and looked as keen to take on the job as they were to instal him. 'Borussia Dortmund wasn't the worst offer you could get,' he joked on arriving.

The PR department at the club lost no time in promoting their new asset, launching a campaign in which Klopp's image towered from billboards all over the city. The sale of season tickets picked up, and then went through the roof. Everybody wanted to be on the Klopp express. Even before the season started the new manager put himself out to talk to staff at the club, fans' representatives, former players. Other coaches would have regarded these duties as an imposition – a drag – but Klopp knew that these people were the lifeblood of BVB. Just as Dortmund believed in Klopp, it was clear from the outset that Klopp believed in Dortmund.

Sometimes he would go beyond the call of duty. A former Dortmund press officer, Josef Schneck, remembers a particular act of kindness. He had happened to mention to Klopp that his mother was about to turn 90.

Klopp asked if he might drop by and congratulate her. Schneck was touched but didn't believe the offer was serious and didn't mention it again. But a few weeks later he was startled when the coach reminded him – your mum's birthday is coming up, give me the address and I'll call in. Cue the big day and who's there to toast the nonagenarian with coffee and cake but Klopp, chatting away with Mrs Schneck and her friends. It was the kind of gesture that came naturally to him.

But it was on the pitch where the new manager's mettle would really be tested. It was one thing to have stamped his authority on the playing style at Mainz; quite another to impose those techniques on the sleeping giant of Dortmund. Would the players accept the high-intensity, high-pressing regime he was there to implement? In a way they had no choice. Klopp didn't do coaching by consent. Either you bought into the programme or you were out. Sebastian Kehl, a holding midfielder, was appointed captain. He recalls how Klopp fundamentally changed the team from a possession-based outfit to one that ran and pressed. The groundwork was done in video sessions combined with long hard yards on the training field. Kehl's own game underwent a revolution: instead of falling back into his own half as soon as Dortmund lost the ball upfield he and his teammates were instructed to press the space in an effort to win the ball back straightaway. If one player pressed and missed, the next had to be ready in support. Doubling up, even tripling up, would give their opponent no time on the ball. The basic strategy was to run the opposition ragged.

The Klopp way required, inevitably, extreme levels of fitness. It also meant that the player profile at Dortmund changed. Younger players were not only more likely to accept the new system but were also better conditioned physically to meet its demands. On top of that was an economic imperative: Dortmund didn't have the cash to spend on prestige signings. Certain members of the BVB old guard were offloaded to trim the wage bill. But Klopp enjoyed building a team. He surprised many by establishing a new central defensive pairing in Neven Subotić and Mats Hummels, both 19-year-olds. Hummels had been a star performer at youth level for FC Bayern, while Subotić had already won his spurs in the Mainz first team. In the previous season Dortmund had shipped 62 goals, more than any other team in the league. That would not happen again under Klopp's watch.

Success did not come overnight. Klopp had always been an optimist but he understood about managing expectations: perseverance would be required of both players and fans. The latter are among the most passionate in the Bundesliga, their noise concentrated in the 25,000 who regularly pack the south stand, the famous and feared 'Yellow Wall'. The highlight of the early part of the season was the Ruhr derby at home to Schalke 04, Klopp's fourth game in charge. It would be a defining moment. Dortmund were 3–0 down on 54 minutes. Somehow they clawed their way back, first through a Subotić goal, then substitute Alexander Frei made it 3–2. With a minute left BVB were awarded a dodgy penalty and, with his manager unable to watch, Frei converted it: 3–3. At the press conference afterwards an exhausted Klopp admitted, 'I've seen wins that haven't felt this good.' The mood suffered a wobble in the autumn with a 2–0 home defeat against Udinese in the UEFA Cup and a 4–1 spanking against Hoffenheim, who played a system like BVB's, only better. 'We need to get where they are now,' said Klopp. 'Tactical behaviour is not like riding a bike, unfortunately. You have to practise, again and again.'

There were other setbacks, though the first half of the season showed decent progress: seven wins, eight draws, two defeats. The resumption in the new year seemed to undo all the good work, with only one win in seven. But Klopp held his nerve and the team rallied, winning eight of the final ten matches, and were unluckily pipped to a European place on the last day of the campaign. In any event sixth felt a lot better than 13th. His second season at Dortmund began like a bad dream, with two heavy defeats, 4–1 to Hamburg and a crushing 5–1 at home to Bayern. Things took a nosedive with another home defeat, this time by a single goal to Schalke, of all teams. After seven league games BVB languished in 15th place, their worst start in 24 years. That it was also their centenary year put the squashed cherry on the cake. Klopp didn't hide. When angry supporters turned up mobhanded at the training ground following the Schalke defeat he got off the team bus and talked to them. His honesty and his willingness to engage impressed the unhappy fans, and after exchanging views for 20 minutes the ugly mood dissolved. The fans went home, having thanked the boss for his time. It was a tactic that might easily have backfired, but Klopp demonstrated not only his grace under pressure but his self-confidence.

He drew deeply on that spirit to wrest them out of the slump. He knew the recipe was more patience, more encouragement, more hard work: nobody else could do it for them. 'Get on the wild ride' was one of his favourite phrases; but 'wild' football needs the underpinning of discipline. In other words, you have to earn the freedom to go nuts. Gradually his young players got the bit between their teeth and returned to winning ways, climbing up the table to fifth. They hung on to it for the remainder of the season. It was the first time the club had qualified for European competition through its league position in seven years.

Interlude: A Confession

When I decided to write a book about Jürgen Klopp it was the story of his transformation of Liverpool FC that excited me. It looked to be a perfect symbiosis: the fascination of a charismatic and inspirational coach and the efflorescence of a football team I'd supported most of my life. Win–win, as it were. I realised of course that any such book would have to cover Klopp's early years, his family, his faith, the Swabian influence, and so on. There would also be an obligation to analyse his career as a player and later as a coach: he hadn't sprung fully formed into the phenomenon of 'Jürgen Klopp' after all. This would mean catching up on a subject – German football – which had up to now been, if not a closed book, then one rarely consulted. Mainz 05, Borussia Dortmund, the last 20 years of the Bundesliga: this would be homework. Except in so far as they were linked to the Life of Klopp I had no interest in them. They would simply be stops on the way towards October 2015 and his arrival at Anfield – where the story *really* began.

That was my thinking as I started out. And I couldn't have been more wrong.

Back in the long ago I remember a girlfriend digging out an album of family photos to show me, and my gaze falling hungrily on pictures of the beloved woman as a girl, a teenager, a student – all the phases of her life that I'd missed. It was more than a feeling of melancholy that oppressed me; it was envy of those people, the siblings and cousins and friends, who had known her in those tender years. I wasn't aware at the time that Philip Larkin, the laureate of lost things, had written a famous poem on this very subject, mourning the woman in the photograph, 'unvariably lovely there', whom he would never know.

Now I wouldn't say that mugging up on Klopp's rise to prominence has left me *distraught* for missing out, but I do find myself wishing I had been along for the ride at the time – in particular the Dortmund years. I have read so much, watched so much footage of the team in action between 2008 and 2015 that I feel, retrospectively, almost a fan of theirs. The players who thrived under Klopp's reign – Hummels, Subotić, Reus, Götze, Kagawa, Lewandowski, Grosskreutz, Şahin, et al. – have come belatedly, heroically alive to me, distant as I am. I have even conceived a love of that black and yellow strip in its various iterations, the trims and chevrons somehow a fitting echo of police incident tape (DO NOT CROSS). I also rejoice to watch Bayern getting beaten, although that was pretty much the case already. And there at the margins the familiar figure of Kloppo, different spectacles, longer hair* but reassuringly the same hyperactive song-and-dance man, sprinting up and down the touchline, pummelling the air. There's a photo

---

* It wasn't only his teeth that Klopp upgraded. The hair transplant he underwent was all over the news in Germany. His beloved protégé Mario Götze, writing in *The Players' Tribune*, recalls bumping into his manager in Düsseldorf during summer 2012. Quite unembarrassed, Klopp told him he was there to see a specialist for a hair transplant. 'He was smiling, telling me all about it – how cool it was going to look and everything. And then as he was leaving, he just gave me a wink and he said, "Mario, don't worry, I will save the phone number." I said, "What do you mean?" He said, "The doctor's number. I'll save it for you. In a few years, you might need it."' Klopp showed off his reconstituted locks at a friendly in Cologne in January. 'Yes, it's true. I had a hair transplant,' he told reporters. 'And I think the results are really cool, don't you?' Instead of trying to hush up his vanity project he joked freely about it, revealing himself again as the living embodiment of what the French call *être bien dans sa peau*.

of him mid-star jump that recalls Pete Townshend in his airborne pomp on stage with The Who.

In truth, I love watching BVB because you can sense Klopp everywhere in their mercury-quick movement, their unity, their unselfish pressing. More than that, you can plot the progression of what was happening at Westfalenstadion to what would happen at Anfield. It's right there – only the names are different. I'm just sorry that I didn't witness the good times first-hand.

Sixth and fifth in his first two seasons wasn't a bad return on the faith invested in him at Dortmund. The vibrations coming out of Signal Iduna Park – the other name of the Westfalenstadion – had been felt throughout the Bundesliga; something major was in the offing. Klopp had by now got together a very fit, very tight squad of young players who followed him 'like Jesus's disciples'. They were players who hadn't yet fulfilled their potential and were eager to prove themselves. 'We knew exactly what the coach wanted us to do,' said Hummels, 'and it was actually fun to play that way.' The 2010–11 campaign did not get off to an auspicious start as BVB lost 2–0 at home to Bayer Leverkusen. Yet this and the final game of the *Hinrunde* – the first half of the season – would be their only two defeats in 17 matches. Astonishingly, they won the other 14 and drew once. Their fleet-footed pressing game had come of age. By January they were 12 points clear and looking likely to go all the way. But Klopp cracked down on premature celebration. 'I couldn't care less about the table,' he said. He took the pressure off his players by insisting that they would take one game at a time: it was the same mantra he would adopt in a similar run-in ten years later, at Liverpool.

In late February 2011 came a crunch fixture away to Bayern. BVB hadn't won in Munich for 20 years, and Bayern, pepped up by an away victory midweek against Inter in the Champions League, were in bullish mood. Their chairman, Uli Hoeness, had predicted victory at the Allianz Arena by a margin of two goals or more. Which he got right – except that it was Dortmund who won, 3–1. Their first goal was signature Klopp, a *Gegenpressing* sucker punch: Grosskreutz nicks the ball off a dozing Schweinsteiger deep in Bayern's half before sliding an immaculate pass into the path of Barrios, who steers it past the advancing keeper. Bayern equalised minutes later, but even with 70 per cent possession they couldn't cope with BVB's incisive running and defending from the front. A curling left-footed beauty from Nuri Şahin and a second-half header from Mats Hummels clinched a famous win. 'It doesn't get any better,' said Klopp, adding that the last time Dortmund triumphed in Munich 'the boys were still being breast-fed'.

With ten games to go it was a huge psychological boost. Bayern had been knocked off their perch, at home, and Hoeness's lame efforts to psych out Klopp were brushed aside. In spite of a 1–0 defeat against Hoffenheim and a draw at home to Mainz Dortmund's march to the *Meisterschaft* was not to be resisted. Klopp had marked ten years in management by reaching the top of the tree. But it was the style as much as the substance of his team's triumph that impressed. They had become champions with a brand of fluid, imaginative football that excited the crowds and made their rivals look very ponderous indeed. When they lifted the trophy in May Klopp said, 'What you realise on a day like this is that in Dortmund football is more than a pleasant distraction, it's the main attraction. For the men and women of this city, and this is something I truly came to understand on Sunday, they're just as much there for BVB in the bad times as they are in times like these.'

That calibre of leadership would be put to the test when the 2011–12 season came around. It's one of the old football truisms that the only thing harder than winning the title is keeping hold of it. The good news for Dortmund was that their squad stayed more or less intact over the summer. Of the regulars only Şahin was tempted away, joining Mourinho's Real Madrid for €10 million on a six-year contract.* The hole he left was filled by 20-year-old İlkay Gündoğan, bought from FC Nürnberg. Klopp sounded an early warning of what lay ahead: 'We're going to have a lot of problems this season,

---

* It wasn't a happy move, and nor was his next one on loan to Liverpool in August 2012. It began well, with three goals in four appearances, but it became apparent that the stately, elegant midfielder wasn't suited to the pace of the Premier League. He moved back to Dortmund via Madrid in January 2013.

that's normal. The next time we lose a game we're going to see what the reaction is.'

He got a glimpse of that reaction sooner than he would have liked. Following a 3–1 win at home to Hamburg on the opening day of the season BVB slumped to a 1–0 defeat at Hoffenheim the following week. In September they lost two on the bounce, to Hertha Berlin and Hannover 96, both 2–1. After six games they had seven points, the worst start to a campaign by defending Bundesliga champions in nearly 30 years. Part of the problem was that Dortmund had to carry the burden of success: when you're top dogs everybody wants to beat you. Teams had got wise to the Klopp press and now defended deeper. The slick movement that characterised their championship season would come at a premium. What's more, they were missing chances; their nimble Paraguayan striker Barrios, who had notched 16 league goals the previous term, was out injured.

As if that wasn't disheartening enough Klopp and his young team were being given a lesson at the high table of the Champions League. Drawn in a group with Arsenal, Marseille and Olympiacos they finished bottom, with four points. The high-energy style that had served them so brilliantly in the Bundesliga was found wanting in Europe, where teams tended to be more streetwise. Their final game in the group at home to Marseille was especially galling: 2–1 up with five minutes to play they somehow conceded not once but twice, the latter a wonder strike from Valbuena on 88 minutes.

On the domestic front, however, things had been quickly set to right. From October 2011 they went on a remarkable run of 28 games unbeaten, and in the meantime found a new spearhead in Robert Lewandowski. After a quiet start to his Dortmund career he now hit his stride, beginning with a hat-trick in a 4–0 drubbing of Augsburg. He would also score the single decisive goal in their victory over Bayern at Signal Iduna Park, a game lent extra gilding by Arjen Robben missing a late penalty and then an open goal. The win moved them six points clear at the top with four games to go. Even then Klopp would sound a note of caution. 'A lot can happen before the end of the season,' he said. Is there an equivalent phrase in German for squeaky-bum time?

In the end they enjoyed a squeakless procession to the title with four straight wins, including a euphoric 2–1 victory away to Schalke. They had amassed 81 points from 34 games, a Bundesliga record at the time. The back-to-back titles were a testament not only to Klopp's tactical supremacy but to his careful man management. In this regard İlkay Gündoğan was a notable beneficiary. At another club the coach might have tried to force an incoming player's development. Instead, Klopp had eased the raw young midfielder into the side by stages, keeping the pressure off him until he was ready to shoulder responsibility. Gündoğan himself later talked of this nurturing approach and ascribed his burgeoning as a player entirely to Klopp. The coach's ability to deal one-to-one with players has become something of a legend. As he said, 'Players are often surprised when I meet them for the first time that I don't talk at all about football.' His reasoning is this: I already know you're a good footballer or we wouldn't be here talking. I want to know what you're like as a human being.

The excitements of 2011–12 were not yet complete. There was still the small matter of the cup final at the Olympic Stadium in Berlin, and the chance for Dortmund to clinch their first-ever Double. Almost inevitably, their opponents were Bayern. They got off to a dream start when Kagawa slotted one after three minutes. Bayern levelled with a Robben penalty before Hummels put them back in front, also from the spot. Then Lewandowski took over and scored a blistering hat-trick, two of them the fault of goalkeeper Neuer, who had a nightmare. The 5–2 scoreline didn't flatter them. 'There were plenty of tricky moments,' Klopp said at full-time, 'but that ice-cold finishing was brilliant. Some of our goals were works of art.' It was BVB's fifth victory on the spin over Bayern and put to bed an extraordinary season. It seemed to mark a changing of the guard, too, the force of Klopp's all-for-one underdogs ousting the Bavarian coalition of individual superstars and massive financial clout. It felt like a victory for romance over business.

The illusion was short-lived. Business has a way of rebooting itself and Bayern, stung by their humiliation in Berlin, began a refurbishment job no other Bundesliga club could dream of affording. In the summer a gigantic spending spree – including a club record of €40 million for Javi Martínez from Atletico Bilbao – announced their intent to squash all-comers. By March the following season Bayern were top with a 17-point lead, and Klopp, understandably narked, pointed out that the Munich Death Star was simply following his own blueprint: 'At the moment it is like what the Chinese are doing in industry: they look at what others do, copy them, and then with more money and players follow a similar path.' The Bayern juggernaut thundered on regardless and claimed the 2012–13 title with a staggering 91 points, ten more than BVB had managed the previous season. They broke a truckload of other records, including the biggest points margin (25) over the second-placed team: Dortmund.

Another sickener, in fact a double whammy, was waiting round the corner. Mario Götze – Super Mario – announced that he was moving to Bayern. He had been with Dortmund since he was nine years old, a favourite son and the epitome of Klopp's youth revolution at the club. At first no one could quite believe it. Klopp told Donald McRae of the *Guardian*, 'It was like a heart attack . . . like somebody had died. I couldn't speak.' He couldn't go out with his wife that night to a film premiere. Götze would be the first major signing by Bayern's new coach, Pep Guardiola. Klopp had a private face-to-face with his departing superstar and told him, 'You're making a mistake.' Too late, the deal was done. And just as they were recovering from the shock the Death Star struck again, this time outrageously poaching BVB's talisman striker Lewandowski. Now where would the goals come from? The mood around Dortmund felt suddenly rather bleak. Klopp had said that Bayern made it their aim to 'copy' their competitors and achieve success by imitation. But this was worse – this was no copy, they had simply blown the bloody doors off and stolen the originals.

Against that unsettled background Klopp brought his Dortmund side to Wembley in May to face Bayern in the 2013 Champions League final: a Bundesliga derby, with chips. Bayern were favourites, though most neutrals were backing BVB. 'We are a club, not a company,' Klopp said with perhaps a touch of asperity. A neutral might favour Bayern, but 'if he wants the new story, the special story, it must be Dortmund'. Alas, Götze, who might have made the final his bittersweet swansong, was injured with a hamstring. The game was fast-paced and intense, with the early chances coming BVB's way. They would rue those misses once Bayern asserted their control in the second half, a Mandžukić goal putting them ahead on the hour. Gündoğan equalised with a penalty eight minutes later, though Klopp was incandescent that the Bayern defender Dante, already on a yellow, wasn't sent off for the foul on Reus. It ended with a slap in the face for Dortmund, and those neutrals, when Robben popped up with an 89th-minute winner. 'We have to respect Bayern's win,' Klopp said afterwards. 'We shouldn't forget that many teams wanted to get to the final, and that Bayern shot half of Europe to pieces on the way here.'

It was a huge disappointment, but he was philosophical. He had known triumph and disaster – Kipling's 'two impostors' – and he had learnt to treat them just the same. The danger now was that more players would follow Götze and Lewandowski out of the Westfalenstadion: Europe's richer clubs would be circling. Might they have their sights on the BVB coach as well?

5. ShanKlopp: An A–Z

A: Anfield

Where else to begin? In autumn 1959 Bill Shankly was approached by Tom Williams, then chairman of Liverpool, with an offer: 'How would you like to manage the best club in the country?' 'Why, is Matt Busby packing up?' Shankly replied. At the time Liverpool were hacking around the Second Division, and Shankly was managing Huddersfield, without a contract. He told Williams he would consider it, though privately he had no doubts about taking the job. He knew the potential of the club. On arriving at Anfield in December he was immediately dismayed by the decrepit condition of the place; there was no watering equipment for the pitch apart from a pipe and a tap in the visitors' dressing room. The training ground at Melwood was 'a sorry wilderness', with an air-raid shelter, an old wooden pavilion and a pitch that looked like a bombsite. In his autobiography he wrote, 'The ground was not good enough for the public of Liverpool and the team was not good enough for the public of Liverpool. The people were thirsting for success. They had been in the doldrums for too long.' The public of Liverpool! I don't suppose Anfield's shabbiness preyed much on the minds of the public who were Everton fans. Shankly set about renovating the stadium and the facilities, determined against penny-pinching: 'Only the best is good enough for Liverpool.' He hated having to persuade the directors not to do things on the cheap, and at times his wrangling with the board nearly prompted him to leave. But he usually got his way.

It's safe to say that the building Jürgen Klopp walked into more than half a century later was a very different set-up. One of my favourite photographs is of him smiling and pointing to the 'THIS IS ANFIELD' sign above the steps towards the tunnel. Together at last. He too would change the *modus operandi* at Anfield, not in the nuts-and-bolts way of Shankly but in the club's culture. He introduced himself to the non-playing staff at the stadium and at Melwood, and then made a point of introducing the staff to the players: they would all be in this together. That sense of mutual loyalty would extend to the crowd on matchdays. When Liverpool lost 2–1 at home to Crystal Palace one month into his tenure Klopp was surprised to see supporters leaving the stadium right after Palace scored their 82nd-minute winner. Where was the famous Anfield Roar? 'I felt pretty alone in this moment,' he confessed at the press conference. 'But we are responsible. Nobody can leave the stadium a minute before the final whistle, because anything can happen.' It was the mildest telling-off, but it perhaps convinced fans to think twice about making an early exit. And given the number of late, late goals LFC would score in the following years Klopp's plea for staying the distance was spot on.

B: Bad Losers

'Show me a good loser and I'll show you a loser.' The line, a quote from NFL coach Vince Lombardi, has always struck me as mean-minded, and pretty juvenile. It sounds like the kind of thing Donald Trump would say. Following the 3–2 Champions League defeat to Atletico at Anfield on 11 March Klopp admitted, 'If I said all the things on my mind I would look like the worst loser in the world,' before taking a swipe at Diego Simeone's negative tactics. 'I don't understand with the quality they have the football they play.' You could understand his frustration. Liverpool played brilliantly on the night, missed a load of chances and were punished by three late counterattacks (and one defensive howler by our goalie, Adrián). But he conceded that Liverpool had had their share of luck in their European adventures of the last two years and he congratulated Atletico on their win. In short he did a very good impression of someone not speaking through clenched teeth* – a bad loser with grace.

---

* A word about those teeth. A short BBC feature, *Klopp, Firmino and Mané: Meet the Dentist Making Liverpool's Stars Shine*, explains the famous 'front rows'. The dentist in question looks like Ross Barkley's Mini-me, though I'm sure he knows what he's doing. Klopp had first visited him to sort out 'problems' with his teeth, in the course of which certain cosmetic improvements were agreed upon. 'It wasn't like I saw Bobby Firmino's teeth and said, "I want them."' They look like a pretty close match, all the same. It seems the entire LFC squad are now clients. Maybe they get a group discount.

Chances are he's still unhappy about that 'fucking loss against Crystal Palace . . .'

Shankly's belief in Liverpool's supremacy was nearly pathological. If his team suffered a defeat he would dismiss it as a flagrant injustice – the referee was hopeless, the opposition was lucky, the pitch was a disgrace. As Hugh McIlvanney wrote, 'His performances in that line were like those of a witch doctor, full of blind faith and incantations.' He magicked away reverses. Alex Ferguson was similarly one-eyed: when Liverpool beat Man Utd 4–1 at Old Trafford in March 2009 (oh, happy day) we utterly outclassed them. Fergie, however, bemoaned their luck and claimed that all four goals came from 'errors'. On that reckoning you could say every goal comes from an error, since every goal technically is preventable. But what joy back then for those Liverpool players when Shankly would target the blame for a defeat on anything but them.

C: Cup Finals

Until recently Klopp seemed afflicted by a cup final hex. In 2012 his Dortmund team had beaten Bayern 5–2 in Berlin to claim the Double, but thereafter he collected a string of losers' medals. He lost two German cup finals in 2014 and 2015, two Champions League finals in 2013 and 2018, and in 2016 lost both the League Cup final to

82

Man City and the Europa League final to Sevilla. Asked about the jinx before Madrid 2019 he was quite relaxed. 'I'm a normal human being, so if I would sit in the room and think it's all about me, I'm the reason, if I would see myself as a loser or whatever, then we all would have a problem, but I don't see it like this.' He squashed his image as a cup-bottler when Liverpool clinched their sixth European Cup on beating Spurs 2–0, a game that might have lived long in the memory had it not been one of the drabbest ever played.

Before Shankly arrived LFC had never won the FA Cup, which back in the '60s still possessed a magical lustre. Recalling the day they beat Leeds 2–1 in the 1965 final at Wembley he describes the reaction with typical understatement: 'Grown men were crying and it was the greatest feeling any human being could have to see what we had done. There have been many proud moments. But that was the greatest day.' He won the FA Cup again in 1974 against Newcastle, a game I recall for Alec Lindsay's wrongly disallowed goal and for the weird spectacle of Shankly on the bench *right next* to the Newcastle manager, Joe Harvey. Has such a seating plan ever been replicated in any stadium since? Watching the game now you can't shake a valedictory feeling. It was Shankly's last-but-one in charge before he sensationally quit in the summer.

D: Drought

It isn't much remarked that the Shankly era featured a seven-year trophy drought. From 1966 to 1973 they won nothing, possibly on account of their ageing squad, though Shankly also hinted at another reason: 'When you have had success it can be a difficult job to motivate yourself. You have done it before, like walking up and down the same road.' After Watford dumped them out of the FA Cup in February 1970 he realised that a team rebuild was unavoidable, and proceeded to ship out a number of senior players. Being Shankly he didn't tell individuals to their face that time was up, he simply left them out. Roger Hunt and Ian St John were among those culled, and deeply resented the manager's silent way with the cut-throat. In his autobiography St John recalls how he discovered his fate one matchday: the teamsheet came around and his name wasn't on it. 'Neither Shankly nor I could change the realities of football, or the ageing process, but he could have shown a little courtesy. He could have taken away some of the rawness of the pain.' Difficult to know how such a great manager could shirk that basic decency. High-handed – or just embarrassed?

The lean years came to an end with the league title of 1972–73 and a UEFA Cup win over two legs against Borussia Mönchengladbach. By a neat symmetry another seven-year drought afflicted the LFC of today. The League Cup victory over Cardiff in 2012 would be the last time a trophy came to Anfield until 2019, when they came along like London buses – the Champions League, the UEFA Super Cup and the FIFA Club World Cup. (I didn't know how much I cared about this last until the final against Flamengo in December: a nail-biting 1–0 win, and maybe Jordan Henderson's greatest game.) 2019 also marked Klopp's first silverware since his Double triumph with Dortmund in 2012 – another seven-year itch scratched.

E: Everton

'I always said we had the best two teams on Merseyside . . . Liverpool and Liverpool Reserves.' I have often wondered how much Everton fans hated Shankly for that celebrated barb. He didn't stop there ('If Everton were playing at the bottom of my garden, I'd pull the curtains'), sniping at them whenever the fancy took him. Perhaps he never forgave Everton for being in the First Division when he took over at Liverpool, then in the Second. Perhaps he just needed an Auld Rival. There is a piercing irony about this antagonism, however, for after Shankly retired and fell out with the board at Anfield one of the clubs that welcomed him was Everton. 'I have been received more warmly by Everton than I have been at Liverpool,' he remarked mournfully. There may have existed on both sides a touch of 'My enemy's enemy is my friend.'

Oddly enough, while watching the Netflix series *Sunderland 'til I Die* I kept thinking of Everton, another huge club with a proud fan tradition and a chaotic history of mismanagement. Sunderland can at least take consolation from their local rival Newcastle also dining on scraps in this era (though dining at the Premier League table rather than plummeting to League One in two seasons). Everton on the other hand have not only endured a trophyless 25 years, they have had to witness the enemy across the park finally getting their act together and winning stuff. Klopp, incidentally, has never lost a Merseyside derby. The last time Everton beat Liverpool was at Goodison, 2–0 in October 2010, during Roy Hodgson's unhappy stewardship. I am old enough to remember the pink *Liverpool Echo* that came out on a Saturday evening, with the teams' results posted in a cartoon on the masthead – Everton represented by the Toffee lady and Liverpool by an Andy Capp-style bloke with a rattle. When I Googled it, however, all that came up was an *Echo* story about Pink, the pop star, playing a live show at Anfield.

F: Fans

If there is one single thing that unites Klopp and Shankly it's their commitment to the fans – and the degree of adoration returned. Both men instinctively grasped that the relationship between a club and its support is a romantic one. Before he came to Anfield Klopp knew from his years at Mainz and Dortmund the near-religious zeal of fandom, but I wonder if even he was a little taken aback by the fervour on Merseyside. In his first few weeks he was bemused by the number of people approaching him for a selfie. ('With all these pictures on Twitter it always looks like I'm in restaurants and bars. I am not that type of guy.') You sense that Klopp loves the fans and enjoys the veneration. But he's too canny to trust it. Football being a 'results business' (yawn) and fate being fickle, the shrewd manager knows the love may not last forever. The trick is to get out at the right moment.

What I hadn't anticipated was the admiring envy Klopp would inspire among outsiders. You can read it on all the fan message-boards. I have lost count of the times non-Liverpool fans have told me how much they'd love 'Jürgen' to be their manager. Not just because he's brilliant at his job, but because he's witty and ebullient and genuinely thrives on club support. Managers, even the great ones, aren't known for spreading happiness.

Shankly was in no doubt as to his priorities. 'Right from the start I tried to show that the fans are the people who matter. You've got to know how to treat them.' Like Klopp's, his rapport with them began early in his career. When manager at Carlisle, instead of writing a letter in the match programme he addressed the crowd on the Tannoy at quarter to three, announcing team changes and asking for vocal encouragement. A public pep talk.

'At a football club there's a holy trinity,' he once said, 'the players, the manager and the supporters.' He added, with lordly disdain, 'Directors don't come into it. They are only there to sign the cheques.' That attitude would come back to bite him.

G: Global Pandemic

As I write this, on Good Friday, 10 April 2020, we are in limbo. Today a record 980 people have died from Covid-19 in the UK, higher than the worst day's toll in Spain. The total number of coronavirus fatalities here stands at 9,016, and figures are expected to climb for the next two weeks. In this context the suspension of sport and the stopped clock of the English Premier League are almost an irrelevance. With the country in lockdown and social-distancing measures being enforced by the police, it's forbidden to have a kickabout in a park, let alone play in a stadium.

That doesn't stop us missing football, and it doesn't stop Liverpool fans wondering nervously about the future. At present we are top of the PL, 25 points ahead, and yet there is talk of the league being voided altogether. Shortly after the announcement of football being closed for business Klopp delivered a statement online to the fans that was calm, compassionate and penetratingly sane. He first of all put football in its place as 'the most important of the least important things in life'.* What matters, he said, is the safety and well-being of society, and if suspending football ensures the health of a single individual then so be it. 'In the present moment, with so many people around our city, the region, the country and the world facing anxiety and uncertainty, it would be entirely wrong to speak about anything other than advising people to follow expert advice and look after themselves and each other.' In an era when experts have been scorned and undermined you felt proud of him for saying that. It was statesmanlike, in contrast to certain utterances from those who were actually *meant* to be statesmen. But the waiting goes on.

The last time the world was gripped by a pandemic, the Spanish flu outbreak of 1918, an estimated 50 million people died from it. Bill Shankly was five years old. In the Lancashire Section of the English League Everton came top, Stoke second, Liverpool third. Football didn't matter then, either.

H: Humour

Shankly's standing as the drollest of all football men was unassailable until Klopp came on the scene. That they should end up managing the same club is fitting:

* A quote that is variously attributed to Arrigo Sacchi, Carlo Ancelotti and Pope John Paul II.

Liverpool loves a wag. But they aren't funny in the same way. Shankly's sense of humour was flinty and combative in the best Scots tradition. He was fast as a gunslinger with a quip, but sometimes what he said owed more to belligerence than wit. On the famous occasion he found Tommy Smith having his leg strapped in the physio's room Shankly told him he wasn't playing anyway, so he could get off the table. An argument ensued, at the end of which Smith said it was his leg and he could do what he liked with it. Shankly replied, angrily, 'It's not your bloody leg. It's Liverpool FC's leg! And you're not bloody playing!' Always scheming to steal a march on the opposition he would go down to their dressing room pre-match to say hello and crack a joke or two. Then he would hurry back to the Liverpool dressing room: 'Christ, I've seen them coming in, boys. They've been out on the tiles! Bobby Moore looks older than me! I'm not joking . . .' With his drill-sergeant's haircut and his guttural Lowland burr Shankly wielded his humour like a weapon, looking to pierce his adversary's defences. And no adversary got his back up more than authority: 'Policemen, bloody useless! They have two on the door of 10 Downing Street and the prime minister still gets out.'

Klopp's humour is gentler, defter, more cosmopolitan: let it not be forgotten that he's being witty in his second language. (He claims to have learnt English from watching the sitcom *Friends*.) If he's this good in a foreign tongue he must be world-class in German.* YouTube has so many compilation clips of him – 'Jürgen Klopp Funny Moments', 'Klopp Top 10 Funny Moments', 'Klopp Funniest Ever' etc. – a non-football person might mistake him for a comedy genius. His press conferences tend to be lively affairs and generally raise more laughs than a professional stand-up would – even the ones he gives in German. Where Shankly's facial expression hardly seemed to change Klopp's is as mobile as an actor's. One of my favourites is his reaction to a rambling, incomprehensible and almost inaudible question from a foreign journalist that ended something like: '. . . (blah blah) it would seem with the same squad like the way you play against Chelsea or are there gonna be any changes?' Klopp listens bemused for a while, then turns to the camera, laughing silently. He then pauses, deadpan, and says, 'Yes.' Cue gales of laughter.

Or how about this beauty, on competing against Bayern Munich: 'We have a bow and arrow and if we aim well, we can hit the target. The problem is that Bayern has a bazooka. The probability that they will hit the target is clearly higher. But then Robin Hood was apparently quite successful.' It's that last sentence which is genius. Having noted the high 'probability' of Bayern hitting

---

* I finally accepted my Klopp obsession when I found myself watching 20-minute excerpts of his press conferences at Dortmund. I don't speak any German, but it doesn't matter: I love the way he teases the journalists and the BVB press officer, Josef Schneck, sitting alongside him. The fun he's having! Or, as Barry Davies famously said, 'Look at his face – just *look* at his face!'

their target, most others would have finished on a note of what-can-you-do resignation. No one but Klopp would have gone upbeat by exampling an English folk hero's guerrilla defiance.

He laughs uproariously at his own jokes, but so would you if you were as funny as him. His sense of comedy is all the more cherishable in the face of Mourinho's slot-mouthed sullenness or Sam Allardyce's charmless northern-business-man-interrupted-at-lunch, or (no kidding) 'Top 5 Hilarious Van Gaal Moments'.

I: Inheritance

When Shankly first arrived at the club he might have installed his own staff. Instead he chose to retain the men who were already there, Reuben Bennett, Joe Fagan and Bob Paisley. It proved to be one of his masterstrokes. Paisley, a physiotherapist and a shrewd tactician, would work at Shankly's side for the next 15 years: Godfather and consigliere of the Boot Room. In his nine years as manager (1974–83) Paisley would outdo his former boss, winning six league titles, three European Cups, three League Cups and a UEFA Cup. A staggering record. Could any other successor to Shankly have done the same? The broadcaster and journalist John Keith has observed that 'nobody could have ignited Liverpool's fire like Shankly, and nobody could have fuelled it like Paisley'.

A photograph of Shankly hangs in Klopp's office – a nod of respect to the heritage, and a good-luck charm.

J: Johnson, Bert

Bert Johnson was the maintenance foreman at Anfield whose idea it was to put a sign over the tunnel to the pitch. He suggested it to the club secretary, Peter Robinson, who then got the OK from the boss. The original sign was to read 'Welcome to Anfield', but Shankly vetoed that. They would *not* be welcoming opponents – they would be reminding them where they stood. So it read: 'THIS IS ANFIELD'. Klopp refused to let his players touch the sign until they had won a trophy. They earned that privilege on 1 June 2019.

K: Keegan, Kevin

I have managed so far in these pages to resist the word 'iconic' – it only came into vogue because it sounds more important than 'famous' – but casting around for a player who could link the Shankly and Klopp eras I'm afraid only iconic will do. It had to be a passionate, heart-on-the-sleeve character whose attachment to LFC is equalled only by the reverence in which he's held by the fans. My first thought was Kenny Dalglish. My second thought was Steven Gerrard. My third thought . . .

Andy Beattie, an LFC scout, had tipped off the management about 'a boy at Scunthorpe' who he believed had massive potential; at the end of the 1970–71 season they signed him for £35,000. It was the deal of the century. Shankly thought so highly of the player that he devoted a whole chapter to him in his autobiography. Kevin Keegan completed the spine of his rebuild, with Ray Clemence in goal and Emlyn Hughes at centre-half, but he was more than that: 'He was the inspiration of the new team,' reckoned Shankly. He was also the first Liverpool player I idolised. When he and John Toshack were playing one-twos all seemed right with the world. Keegan had a habit of scoring vital goals – the astonishing volley-lob against Leicester in the 1974 FA Cup semi, the two goals in the final against Newcastle, a goal in each leg of the 1976 UEFA Cup final against Bruges. But it was his all-round game, nipping about like an electrified ferret, radiating nervous energy, that makes me think of him as a Klopp-type player. Incredibly fit, always willing, he was the talisman who worked his socks off for the team. (Bobby Firmino, we salute you.) When he announced his intention to leave Anfield in 1977 I couldn't believe it. Why would a figure so beloved at Liverpool want to go and play in Europe – in Germany of all places? At the time his leaving shocked me far more than Shankly's, but of course it was different: Keegan was a man looking yonder, while Shankly was a man looking back.

As a creature of temperament, however, Keegan was more interesting than we knew. There had been moments, flashpoints, such as his dismissal for fighting with Billy Bremner in the hotly contested 1974 Charity Shield at Wembley, that indicated trouble ahead. (Aggro at the *Charity Shield*, for God's sake – the spare bin lid of football silverware.) Keegan, having been punched twice and thrown none himself, angrily tore off his shirt as he walked – 'This is a face of English football that we do not want to see,' said Barry Davies, sternly. Wrong. We all lapped it up.

On signing for Newcastle in 1982, following his time at Hamburg and Southampton, Keegan was an instant hero on Tyneside. On the day he retired and was airlifted away, still in his kit, by helicopter, he was a demigod. By the time he came back to manage the club eight years later in 1992 he was, essentially, the Messiah. Like Klopp at Mainz, he saved the club from relegation in his first season. The next he took them up to the Premier League, playing a buccaneering brand of football that was Keegan all over. By February of the 1995–96 season Newcastle were 12 points clear at the top, and the pressure of expectation was higher than a suicide jump off the Tyne Bridge.

You know what's coming next. Of all the great rants I've heard nothing has ever surpassed for hysteria – or hilarity – the magnificent Keegan Meltdown of April 1996. It's football's equivalent of Peter Finch in *Network* ('I'm mad as hell and I'm not going to take this any more!'). Watching the interview again (as I often do) the curious thing is his relative calm at first. Ferguson's disobliging comments about Notts Forest possibly throwing the game to Newcastle plainly irked him, but he was still in control when Keys, in the Sky studio, suggested it was all part of the 'psychological battle' – and Keegan loses it right there. Here is the full text: '. . . *No!* When you do that with footballers, like he said about Leeds, and when you do things like that about a man like Stuart Pearce – I'm, I've kept really quiet. But I'll tell you something – he went down in my estimation when he said that. We have not resorted to that. But I'll tell you – you can tell him now, he'll be watching it – we're still fighting for this title, and he's got to go to Middlesbrough and get something,* and . . . and I'll tell you honestly, I will love it if we beat them – *love it!*' When you try this at home be sure to remember the finger-jabbing and the tone of hoarse indignation. And do wear a pair of outsize headphones.

Strange to say, the reaction to it was not wholly derisive. Roy Keane later said that he regarded the outburst as proof of Keegan's passion for the cause. I imagine Shankly would have thought the same. Blowing a gasket (aka 'the hairdryer') is an occupational hazard of the football manager. No, more like a contractual requirement. 'The gaffer hit the roof . . .' is no less than a fan would demand of his leader. The wise gaffer, though, knows to keep his tantrums in-house. To put it another way, I hope Klopp never does a Keegan – because it will be a sure sign that the end is nigh.

---

* Man Utd did indeed 'get something' at Middlesbrough – a 3–0 win, followed by the league title. Newcastle were second, four points behind.

L: Late Goals

The great teams always seem able to nick one in the nick of time, and in the last couple of years Liverpool have turned the knack into an art. (May we call it the nick-knack?) One would like to think this is down to Klopp's instruction to 'keep going to the last minute', but the way he reacted to Divock Origi's 96th-minute derby winner – tearing onto the pitch to bearhug Alisson, jumping around like David Pleat in his relegation-escape dance – suggested he was as surprised as anyone by Div's alert poaching.* More recently there was Milner's 90+5-minute pen to beat Leicester; the comeback at Villa, 1–0 down for most of the game until Mané brilliantly set up Robertson for the equaliser then scored the injury-time winner; Firmino's last-gasp winner against Monterrey in the Club World Cup semi. This is the stuff of 'mentality giants', the team that week by week refuses to accept not winning.

Shankly regarded late goals for his team as practically a matter of entitlement. He would tell his players that the longer the game wore on the more jittery the opposition became – 'and all of a sudden – boof! We had scored another goal.' Once they were losing 2–1 to West Ham at Upton Park. In the final minutes Shankly had left the dugout and gone downstairs to brood, unaware that

---

* One question about that derby goal: did the assist go to Virgil van Dijk for his woeful sliced waft onto the bar or was it to Jordan Pickford for his fingertip effort to keep the ball in play?

Keegan had equalised with the last kick of the game. Phil Thompson recalls the team returning to the dressing room at the final whistle, all smiles at having secured an unlikely point. The boss stood there glowering like Zeus with his thunderbolt: 'You should never lose to a team like that,' he shouted, and was making the walls shake with his outrage when Bob Paisley told him of the last-minute equaliser. It was a draw, Bill! They say that Shankly blushed, though it's hard to imagine. 'Great result, lads,' he said instantly, 'you deserved it.'

M: Money

When Klopp was manager at Mainz he and the chairman, Christian Heidel, had an annual salary meeting: the figure was always agreed upon with a handshake. It later emerged he was the best-paid manager in the second division. 'And he wasn't a pauper in the first division either,' says Heidel, who never quibbled – he knew what an asset he had. When other clubs tried to lure him away Klopp would laugh at the money they were offering, 'because no one realised how much we were paying him. Seven figures. There were many Bundesliga coaches who didn't make that.' When he moved to Liverpool he was reported to be earning about £7 million a year. In December 2019 he signed a new contract at £15 million a year. I don't think there's a Liverpool fan who would say he isn't worth it. 'Money isn't the most important thing. It is important, of course. I am not Mahatma Gandhi.'

In his autobiography Shankly doesn't say how much he was on at Liverpool but he recounts with some asperity the arguments he had with the board about getting money to buy players. There was a severe reluctance to spend. Only when Eric Sawyer from Littlewoods joined the board did the purse-strings start to loosen – 'a man of vision,' Shankly called him, meaning someone prepared to stump up the cash. When he proposed buying Ian St John and Ron Yeats the directors baulked at the cost, but Sawyer stepped in and said, 'We cannot afford *not* to buy them.'

Shankly himself was prepared to put his hand in his pocket. During his tenure at Carlisle (on £14 a week – 'top money') the team were passing through Doncaster on the way to play Lincoln when he spotted a sports shop, stopped the coach and went in to buy a new set of kit. The team played in it that afternoon. 'They were hard but happy days.'

N: Novels

It's the occasional fate of larger-than-life types that they end up in a novel. Perhaps only fiction can make sense of them. In *Red or Dead* David Peace recreated Shankly as a monument, if not a monomaniac. It comprises a minutely detailed account of his years at Anfield, couched in a prose that becomes incantatory, almost biblical. Peace had already put a football manager centre-stage in his 2006 novel *The Damned Utd*, the story of Brian Clough's ill-starred 44-day reign at Leeds. That too was a record of pain and loss, but in terms of mad-eyed obsession *Red or Dead* leaves it for dust. So deeply involved is this novel in stats and match reports you may sometimes mistake what you're reading for a lonely fan's scrapbook of LFC in the years 1959 to 1974. It dramatises real-life encounters between Shankly and the prime minister Harold Wilson, tracing the parallels between running a football club and leading a government. The implication is that these two were soulmates, tough and canny socialist role models they don't make them like any more. When Shankly was offered his own show on Radio City Liverpool he agreed on the condition that his first guest would be Wilson. Peace's narrative, encompassing even the humdrummery of the retired Shankly at his household chores ('Bill picked up the plates. Bill walked over to the sink. Bill put the plates in the sink. Bill walked back over to the kitchen table' etc.) is bravely *sui generis*, a witches' brew of raw feeling, driven men and hard lines. In an otherwise rave review for the *Guardian* Mark Lawson admitted the novel was 'unlikely to be grabbed as the monthly choice of book groups even in the Anfield and Huyton areas'.

Klopp has also made an appearance in modern fiction, under the guise of a *wunderkind* film director in *Eureka*, a 2017 novel by . . . me. It happened like this. I was writing a story about a mystery film being shot in London during the summer of 1967, catching the same wave as the Antonioni film *Blow-Up* and the just-released *Sgt Pepper's Lonely Hearts Club Band*. It's at heart a romp, based upon the screenwriter's misadventures in sex and drugs, and his friendship with the oddball German hired to direct the film. I planned to base the latter on the filmmaker Rainer Werner Fassbinder, but having read his biography, *Love is Colder Than Death*, I began to have doubts. A prolific and dazzling star of the new German cinema, Fassbinder led a life of gangsterish excess, a dark-hued, drug-addled pageant of emotional cruelty and exploitation aided and abetted by an infamous entourage of hangers-on. The writer Ian Penman neatly described him as 'an inconceivable amalgam of Joe Orton, Jonathan Miller and Sid Vicious'. He died of an overdose in 1982, aged 37.

Tempted as I was, his grim-and-bear-it presence would have unbalanced the tone of the book. I didn't fancy living with such bleakness, and I sensed that the reader wouldn't either. So keeping a pinch of Fassbinder I remodelled my character on two other Germans, essentially benign but with a lightning streak of craziness. One was Werner Herzog, the director of *The Enigma of Kaspar Hauser*, *Nosferatu* et al. And the other was Jürgen Klopp, whose charisma and intensity felt exactly right for the part. His name would be Reiner Werther Kloss: see what I did there? Klopp's famous quote about Mats Hummels's lay-off from injury ('We will wait for him like a good wife waiting for her husband who is in jail') gave me the idea for an entire scene at a casting confab. The director was a lot of fun to write – an off-the-wall visionary, a huge Beatles fan, and something of a firestarter. I imagine the only aspect that his real-life model might object to is Reiner's lifelong support, like Fassbinder's, of Bayern Munich. *Eureka* had some good reviews and pretty indifferent sales. But I was pleased to have put Klopp in it.

O: OBE

I can't tell you how disappointing it is to see those letters after Shankly's name. You get why other celebrities might fall for the meretricious bauble of an honour; they are the kind of people who believe that a seal of public approbation actually matters. But not Bill Shankly. He was no toady to the British Empire, felt no need to bow and scrape to royalty. He was his own man. I dream an alternative scenario in which he describes how he got the call from the Palace: 'Eer . . . a gentleman telephoned asking if I was free to attend a ceremony with Her Majesty on such-and-such a date. I looked in my diary and said, "I'm sorry, son, I'm busy that morning. Reserves game." He came back, asked me if I knew what an *honour* I was being paid. I said, "Tell you the truth, son, there's only one honour I ever *craved*, which was to manage Liverpool Football Club. And I've got that one."'

Me and my older brother Mike (left) in our garden in Huyton, 1969. Or was it 1929? (*Author*)

Me in the Celtic kit, with Mike (right) and younger brother Pete (left), in Calderstones Park, 1972. I have no memory of wearing those white boots. (*Author*)

Young Jürgen and his father, Norbert, on a visit to Bad Kreuznach in 1975. (*Hartmut and Ulrich Rath*)

Ouch. Klopp and Mainz teammate Jürgen Kramny put the boot into the unfortunate Zlatan Bajramović of FC St Pauli. (*Getty*)

Showing his light touch with referees. Just don't make him angry. (*Offside/Witters*)

Mainz man. On the way to perfecting his Pete Townshend star jump. (*Getty*)

Joe Cool. Klopp in shades and flower garland, with president Hans-Joachim Watzke (left) and sporting director Michael Zorc (right). (*Martin Davidsen*)

Celebrating his second Bundesliga title win in May 2012. (*Getty*)

Together at last. Touching the most famous football sign in the world. (*Getty*)

9 October 2015. The Kloppmeister has landed. (*Getty*)

'Very erotic voice, by the way, the translator . . . Again please!' (*Shutterstock*)

7 May 2019. Liverpool players celebrate Divock Origi's second goal that puts them 4–0 up against Barcelona. Maybe the cheekiest goal ever scored in the Champions League, from the greatest ever corner. (*Getty*)

That night in Madrid. Tears of joy with Hendo. (*Getty*)

Der Bumps. (*Shutterstock*)

The Klopp roar. Note assistant Željko Buvać's more muted applause. (*Getty*)

22 July 2020. The Premier League trophy is ours at long last. Anfield almost empty, but the joy is unconfined. (*Getty*)

Alas, even Shankly, man of the people, was suscepti-
ble to the vanity of government-approved recognition.
I recall certain LFC fans doing their nut on Ferguson
getting a knighthood after Shankly and Bob Paisley had
been denied. Ye gods! To appreciate the tawdriness of the
title only consider the stripe of men who have accepted
one: Sir Geoffrey Boycott. Sir Richard Branson. Bono.
And that's just the Bs. George Bernard Shaw got it right:
'Titles distinguish the mediocre, embarrass the superior,
and are disgraced by the inferior.'

Klopp is of course not eligible for an honour, but even
if he were I like to think he'd laugh at the idea. He strikes
me as a man who knows that gentility is not to be found
in birth, or wealth, or title. The only gentility that matters
is gentility of the soul.

P: Promotion

Even today Klopp calls Mainz's first promotion his greatest ever achievement. Because it was the unlikeliest? His
team was forged in his own image as a player – passionate,
ever-willing, but limited. It's a testament to teamwork that
he rallied this quite average bunch of players to heights
they'd never dreamed of scaling before. Like Klopp in
2001–03, Shankly spent his first two seasons at Anfield
narrowly missing promotion. He managed it at the third
attempt, in 1961–62, winning the Second Division title with

62 points. His centre-half Ron Yeats called it the proudest moment of his career: 'Without that nothing else would have happened . . .' At a shareholders' meeting Shankly and the team were presented with 'cigarette boxes' for winning promotion.* He announced, 'Next time we come back here for presents we will have won the First Division.' I wonder what their reward was then – cigars?

Q: Quitting

The old showbiz adage 'Leave 'em wanting more' is a sound one. The fans may be heartbroken but their memories of you will be untarnished. The tragedy of Shankly's retirement is that *he* was the one left wanting more. When he announced he was quitting Liverpool in the summer of 1974 there was widespread shock. 'Whilst you love football, it is a hard, relentless task . . . So I had to say I was retiring.' Did he secretly imagine that the Anfield board would beg him to stay? If he did, the bluff backfired. After all the sniping he'd done some directors were glad to see the back of him. In his autobiography you can hear the regret in his voice: 'I still wanted to help Liverpool, because the club had become my life.' It has become a famous sad story that Shankly in retirement

---

* Klopp would have been happy enough with that: he's still a smoker. Jamie Carragher once suggested that the reason Klopp is often seen sprinting down the tunnel as soon as the half-time whistle blows is his urge for a crafty cigarette.

began to turn up at Melwood, near his home, and join in the training. The players naturally addressed him as 'boss', which put the actual boss, Bob Paisley, in a deeply awkward position. Behind the scenes the sundering perhaps involved no more than a quiet word, but reports began to emerge that Shankly had been banned from the training ground and that the club and its greatest manager had fallen out. Hurt by the rejection he spent the first Saturday afternoon of the new season at Goodison Park* while Liverpool were playing Luton.

When the board did eventually try to make amends and invited him to the second leg of the 1976 UEFA Cup final in Bruges they put him in a different hotel from the one used by the official party. Shankly felt the insult. It was a parting of the ways badly handled on both sides. Nowadays he would be regarded as an asset and honoured with a presidential role, like Dalglish. One has to wonder all the same: if Shankly had stayed on would he have achieved as much as Paisley did in the next nine years? Age and fatigue may have told against him (he was 60 when he resigned) though it plainly didn't hold back Ferguson when he reversed his decision to retire at United in 2001. Shankly never got to find out. He quit prematurely, and he knew it.

On leaving Dortmund in 2015 Klopp had signed off with his least successful season at the club. A wave of injuries, the

---

* Paisley, asked what Shankly was doing that day, replied, 'He's trying to get right away from football. I believe he went to Everton.'

departure of Götze and the captain Hummels's loss of form all played their part in a drastic slump. Halfway through the season BVB lay 17th, with the relegation alarm bells ringing. As the gloom descended Klopp became more fractious with the media, snapping at questions in an uncharacteristic mood of hostility. Results picked up and lifted them to safety, but in Europe Dortmund were dumped out of the Champions League by Juventus. Something had to give, and in April Klopp held a press conference to announce his departure in the summer. He said that he no longer felt he was 'the right coach for this extraordinary club', and given their relationship 'one big head needed to roll – mine'. The shock was palpable, yet the affection between him and CEO Watzke remained. They shared a hug before the cameras. A divorce, or maybe a conscious uncoupling. His leave-taking in front of the fans at Signal Iduna Park in May was positively Wagnerian.

He had managed the club for seven years, the same as he had at Mainz. If he were to follow that pattern it would mean his leaving Liverpool in 2022, though his contract at Anfield runs till 2024. In view of the pressure maybe seven years is all he can give to the job. I hope not.

R: Race

On Monday 1 June the Liverpool squad were photographed 'taking the knee' around the centre-circle at Anfield, a gesture of protest at the death of George Floyd, killed by police officers while under arrest on a street in Minneapolis. It was also a gesture of support for the Black Lives Matter campaign, which gathered momentum across America in mass protests not seen since the Civil Rights movement of the 1960s. When the Premier League resumed on 17 June at Villa Park, the Aston Villa and Sheffield United players also took the knee in a concerted demonstration of solidarity. The shirts on the backs of all PL players bore witness to Black Lives Matter. Football has made itself part of the movement. Race is the only issue of 2020 that has competed with coronavirus as front-page news: it's still *the* issue in the game today.

The Liverpool players' gesture was their own idea, not the club's, though we can be certain that Klopp gave it his full approval. Quite apart from the humanitarian aspect of the protest one imagines he would delight in the simple fact of players taking responsibility, and doing the right thing. Elite footballers get plenty of stick for supposedly living in a bubble; here is evidence that they are just as alive to the historical moment.

Klopp, citizen of the world, has professed great admiration of African-born players – he was a particular fan of the Ghanaian striker Tony Yeboah* when he played for Eintracht Frankfurt in the 1990s – though he has also admitted a serious frustration with losing players

---

* Scorer of possibly the greatest Premier League goal LFC ever conceded, for Leeds, August 1995. The dip on that volley!

mid-season to the Africa Cup of Nations. It became a factor in transfer policy. Yet that didn't prevent LFC signing Mané, Salah and Naby Keïta between 2016–18, successively breaking the African transfer record each time.

In 1974, the year Shankly resigned, 16-year-old Howard Gayle joined the youth team at Liverpool. He signed professional terms with the club in 1977, the first black player ever to do so. It makes you wonder. This city has one of the largest black communities in Europe. LFC was founded in 1892. Is it likely that *not one* black footballer in all that time was good enough to wear the shirt? Gayle didn't make his full debut until 1980, though his name will be forever enshrined for his brilliant cameo when he came on as sub in the European Cup semi-final against Bayern in April 1981. In those benighted days he suffered unimaginable abuse, from the terraces and, notably, from his teammate Tommy Smith.[*]

S: Socialism

Given his birthplace and background Shankly was always likely to be a socialist, and at Anfield he expressed it as an article of faith: 'The socialism I believe in is everybody working for the same goal and everybody having a share in the rewards. That's how I see football, that's how I see life.'

[*] Gayle discusses Smith's antagonism in his autobiography, *61 Minutes in Munich*.

A romantic definition – true socialism is always romantic – and well suited to the tough working-class city he made his home. His friendly association with the Labour prime minister Harold Wilson was good PR for both men, and would have been noted by the fans. The supporters' union formed in 2010 to counter the boardroom piracy of Hicks and Gillett was named, righteously, The Spirit of Shankly. But it's worth remembering that even in the more innocent era of the 1960s football was a business operating on market principles. Shankly, an ex-serviceman, was the 'boss' who wielded power over his charges, and at times did so with apparently no more sentiment than a factory owner or a foreman. Socialism needs its leaders, but he was more benign despot than principled egalitarian. You wonder what Ian St John thought of the all-for-one-and-one-for-all credo after Shankly dumped him without explanation.

Klopp has never been afraid to declare himself a socialist. 'I'm on the left, of course. I believe in the welfare state. I'm not privately insured. I would never vote for a party because they promised to lower the top tax rate.' So it would be interesting to know his thoughts on the Fenway Sports Group's initial response to the global pandemic. In 2019 the LFC chief executive, Peter Moore, on being asked what made the club great, had invoked the spirit of Shankly: 'Even today, when we talk about business, we ask ourselves, "What would Shankly do?"' Cut to the crisis of April 2020 and LFC has chosen to piggyback the government's emergency compensation scheme and furlough its non-playing staff, thus saving about £1 million. This from a club that made a pre-tax profit of £42 million in 2018–19, with an annual wage bill of £310 million. What would Shankly have done? Not that, for starters. Spurs and Newcastle also took the furlough option, but we knew already what manner of men Levy and Ashley were.

Following an outcry Fenway quickly reversed its decision via a mealy-mouthed 'apology'. But the damage was done. In *The Times* Tony Cascarino condemned Liverpool's opportunism and suggested that it would be a turning-point in relations between the manager and his employers: 'It might take a few seasons, but when Klopp and Liverpool do eventually part the brief adoption of furlough will come to be seen as the moment the relationship began to sour.' Klopp had joined Liverpool because it was a special club, different from the rest. In the words of that much-mocked slogan, 'This means more'. In the light of Fenway's original decision it should be amended: 'This means more $'. We may want to believe that LFC is a 'socialist' club, but the people who own it sure as hell aren't socialists…

T: Transfer Policy

. . . and yet our American overlords cannot be accused of stinting on money for transfers. This is the trade-off between integrity and success that fans must live with. When a thrusting capitalist enterprise takes on the running of your club you may feel relieved once they 'make funds available' to buy players. But don't be shocked when they also behave like a thrusting capitalist enterprise.

Recruitment has bedevilled various managers at Liverpool, and to consider the roll call of purchases since 1990 (total: £1.275 billion) is to sup full with horrors. I won't name names[*] – you know who they are. The best signing Fenway Sports have made since arriving at Anfield is, unquestionably, Klopp himself. Everything good about the last five years has flowed from him. Quite apart from his leadership he has shown a readiness to delegate responsibility for transfers to his backroom people. He doesn't make a song and dance about wanting a particular player, unlike, say, Rafa Benítez did when he was determined to offload Xabi Alonso in order to buy Gareth Barry. (Go figure.) In co-operation with FSG president Mike Gordon, sporting director Michael Edwards, head of recruitment Dave Fellows and chief scout Barry Hunter, Klopp has brought in players who have made a vital difference. Some of them are the finished article (Sadio Mané, £30m), some bristling with potential (Andy Robertson, £8m). One vintage model came for free: James Milner was actually a Rodgers signing in summer 2015, but Klopp was quick to appreciate the engine and reliability of this astonishing player. But, to say it again, it's the spine that matters, and

---

[*] Oh all right then. El Hadji Diouf. Paul Konchesky. Christian Poulsen. And Iago Aspas simply for taking the worst-ever corner at Anfield (vs Chelsea 27/4/14).

who now would count Mo Salah (£43.9m), Virgil van Dijk (£75m) or Alisson Becker (£65m) as anything other than a bargain?

Back in 1960 when Shankly was new at Anfield the first player he tried to sign was Jack Charlton. But Leeds wanted more than the parsimonious board at LFC was willing to pay. Knowing that a top-of-the-range goalscorer and centre-half were a *sine qua non*, Shankly made sure the following year to sign Ian St John (£37,500) and Ron Yeats (£30,000). With Tommy Lawrence in goal he had the spine of his first great Liverpool team. He told a director at the time, 'These players will not only win us promotion – they will win us the Cup as well.' They did not let him down.

U: Uncanny

Certain teams not only take on an aura of invincibility, they begin to believe in it themselves. Shankly's burning sense of conviction impressed itself so deeply on his players that they felt like winners before a whistle had been blown. Of his '70s team he said, 'We got to the point where we knew we would win, just as we did with our first great team. We would have been playing for only ten minutes when I would know we were going to win.' Klopp created the same feeling of certainty among his Dortmund players. Interviewed by Raphael Honigstein in his Klopp biography, İlkay Gündoğan says the team went into every game believing they would win: 'We didn't steal the points, we knew: they have no chance against us. One game, against Köln, we were 1–0 down at half-time, no one knew why. We won 6–1. We were so good that it didn't matter if the opposition took the lead.'

V: Van Dijk, Virgil

When Shankly signed Ron Yeats he called a press conference to show off his new acquisition. 'I got all the press boys and said, "Go on, walk around him. He's a colossus!"' I feel he might have indulged a similar admiration of our current man-mountain Virgil van Dijk.* You may recall the hoo-ha around VVD's signing for £75 million in January 2018, the most expensive player in Liverpool's history and a then world-record fee for a defender. Klopp played down the extravagant price tag: 'If you want to sign a player the last thing I think about is the price, to be honest. That's not because I like to throw money around, we are only thinking about the player.' He added, helplessly, 'That's the market, that's the world.'

From the moment he scored the winner on his debut against Everton in the FA Cup van Dijk's time at

---

* And the latest in our regular raids upon the personnel at Southampton. I sometimes wonder where we'd be without their Saintly willingness to sell – no Virge, no Mané, no Lallana, no Clyne, no (um) Lovren.

Liverpool has felt like a romance, a love whose month is ever May. His strength, his positional awareness, his calm under pressure and his near-superhuman resistance to injuries have been essential in making Liverpool the hardest team in the league (the world) to beat. As the saying goes, 'Attack wins you games, defence wins you titles.' One other thing: he has markedly improved the other players around him, in particular his central defensive partners (Joe Gomez could be our Virgil 2.0 in years to come). Like Klopp, he has become the envy of non-Liverpool fans – who wouldn't wish they had him in their team? 'Old-school defending with a modern twist,' said Vincent Kompany, who rates van Dijk as the best ever Premier League defender.

And since we're here, let me briefly reminisce on our favourite Virge moment. 31 March 2019 at Anfield, against Spurs, 85 minutes gone, stuck at 1–1 and we are under the cosh. A sudden breakaway for them, two-against-one, Sissoko in possession looking to feed Son on his right. But the *one* is Virgil, who holds and holds, blocking the pass to Son and forcing Sissoko to take the chance on himself. Which he blazes over. A certain goal saved by a player's defensive wiliness – and he didn't even touch the ball. Skills! Martin Keown, who knows about defending, remarked, 'You will not find it in any coaching manual.' Well, apart from the manual written by VVD, whose first rule is 'They shall not pass.'

W: Wives

Shankly met his wife Agnes – Ness, as she was known – at the end of the war when they were stationed at the same RAF camp in Scotland. Unlike him she was quiet and unassuming, and had no interest in football. That didn't stop the groom taking her to a Preston reserve match on their wedding day. He doesn't mention that in his auto-biography. Indeed Ness remains a shadowy figure in the story, even though he describes meeting her as 'one of the most important events in my life'. It's fair to assume that marriage to a football boss back then was tough going, and to a football boss like Shankly it may have been tougher still. When Shankly was in crisis over retirement she asked him, 'Are you sure you want to do that?' The sentences that follow are curious: 'She didn't want me to do any-thing that I didn't want to do – and this didn't help me. I suppose I wanted her to say, "Now is the time."' It seems he hoped the decision would be taken out of his hands, but Ness, used to her role on the marital equivalent of a subs' bench, couldn't advise him.

Klopp has been married twice. He and his first wife Sabine had a son, Marc, who was a professional footballer. In 2005 Klopp married Ulla Sandrock, whom he had met at a bar in Mainz. She would become known as 'the First Lady of the Bundesliga'. Formerly a teacher and social worker in Nairobi, she retrained as a child psychologist – perhaps the ideal job for someone married to a football coach. She also writes children's books. Her novel *Tom and the Magic Football* was published in 2008: 'It's like Harry Potter but about football,' said Klopp, adding in apparent relief, 'There's no flying on his fucking stick.' (Did they use that for a blurb?) Some newspapers reported that when at Dortmund he was sounded out for the job at Man Utd, but his wife advised him against it. If so, hats off to Mrs Klopp: we are forever in your debt.

X: XXX, Or The Love That Dare Not Speak Its Name

There are no gay footballers in the British game. Does anyone seriously believe that? While other sportspeople have come out, often to public approval, in football it's still the last taboo. The tragedy of Justin Fashanu has cast a long shadow. In Shankly's day the prospect of a homosexual footballer was not only unthinkable – until the Sexual Offences Act of July 1967 it was unlawful. Now we are supposed to be living in more enlightened times; there are gay supporters' groups and campaigns against homophobia and a hopeful spirit of live and let live. We hear occasional rumours that some footballer is about to come out . . . and then it all goes silent again.

So it's cheering to know that even in this atmosphere of dread one manager can defy the unspeakable. The scene: Klopp is at a pre-match presser ahead of a Champions League game against PSG. He's listening via earpiece to a notably husky (male) voice translating a question, and he flashes that toothsome smile before addressing the camera: 'Very erotic voice by the way, the translator . . . Congratulations . . . Wow!' The laughter in the room is just subsiding when he adds, 'Again, please!' – and cracks up, Kloppishly. Can you imagine any other Premier League manager making that joke? Yes, of course it's 'bantz', and no, it doesn't make him a crusader. But even his pretending to be turned on carries an implication: it's OK for a man to fancy another man. In the end that might give more heart to a young footballer in the closet than any amount of anti-homophobia initiatives. Since the clip was posted on YouTube in November 2018 it has had nearly 200,000 views.

Y: 'You'll Never Walk Alone'

Gerry and the Pacemakers made pop history when their first three singles went to number one. The third of them was destined for the ages. 'You'll Never Walk Alone', from the Rodgers and Hammerstein musical *Carousel*, might have sounded rather hymnal to young Merseybeat fans, but on the Kop they loved an American show tune. The story goes that Gerry Marsden presented Shankly with a recording of the song during a pre-season coach trip in the summer of 1963. 'Gerry, my son,' Shankly said, 'I have given you a football team, and you have given us a song.' On its release in October it was immediately adopted as the Anfield theme. When Shankly guested on *Desert Island Discs* just before the Liverpool–Leeds FA Cup final in 1965 he chose 'You'll Never Walk Alone' as his eighth record.

So damn me for a heretic, but I don't like the song. I never have. This in spite of my conviction that Oscar Hammerstein II is a genius, by the way. There are songs of his – 'All the Things You Are', 'Don't Ever Leave Me', 'The Song is You', 'My Favourite Things', 'Some Enchanted Evening' – I would walk through a storm for. But not that one. The mawkishness of it is heightened by its placement in the draggy finale of *Carousel*, with its interminable dream ballet and pious message-mongering. The theatre critic Eric Bentley wrote: 'I refuse to be lectured by a musical comedy scriptwriter on the education of children, the nature of the good life and the contribution of the American small town to the salvation of souls.' Eric, I hear you.

And yet . . . when Anfield is in full voice, you can't imagine them singing anything else. In his excellent book about Liverpool and its music* Paul Du Noyer wrote, 'If Rodgers and Hammerstein had sat down, all those years previously, and deliberately tried to write an anthem for Liverpool and its people, they could not have come up with anything better.' On the night we beat Barcelona 4–0

---

* *Liverpool, Wondrous Place: Music from the Cavern to the Capital of Culture* (Virgin Books).

Klopp, his players and his staff stood linked together in a row, gazing up at the Kop as the love poured down, and the song came into its own. A communion of souls. That was when I understood how it moved people to tears. It was one of the noblest sights, and sounds, Anfield has ever witnessed.

Z: Zero

The number of times either Bill Shankly (Carlisle Utd, Grimsby Town, Workington, Huddersfield Town, LFC) or Jürgen Klopp (FSV Mainz 05, Borussia Dortmund, LFC) has been sacked as manager.

6. No More Heroes

'Klopp's your hero,' says my wife when she finds me googoo-eyed at yet another Klopp clip on my screen. But isn't it rather unbecoming for a man of my age (56) to have heroes? The idea seems juvenile, a throwback to the school playground and pin-ups on your bedroom wall. It seems to me that it's only in the narrow prison yard of adolescence when you *need* heroes – when you long for the transcendent. My earliest, as previously mentioned, were Celtic players, before my allegiance 'moved south' to Liverpool, where Keegan and Toshack and Peter Cormack (a good-looking Scottish midfielder) became the names I thrilled to. Who else mattered back then? The Beatles, of course. Their music was the soundtrack to our family life in the early 1970s – I can barely recall a holiday without 'the red album' (1962–66) or 'the blue album' (1967–70) playing in the car – and though later I became interested in them as individuals, at the time John, Paul, George and Ringo were simply an entity – 'visible powers of nature', like his parents were to the young John Ruskin.

I daringly branched out from The Beatles, aged eight, when I fell for Marc Bolan – T. Rex's 'Metal Guru' was the first single I ever bought, at Woolworth's on Church Street. Then, via Bolan and Mott the Hoople's 'All the

Young Dudes'* I graduated to David Bowie. Like everyone else I remember his performance of 'Starman' on *Top of
the Pops* when he draped his arm suggestively around Mick
Ronson, but the song from that era which really obsessed
me was 'Quicksand', the strange ballad that closed side
one of *Hunky Dory* (1971). It was a song in which Bowie
addressed the limits of comprehension, the anxiety of being
and his intimations of the beyond. It namechecked Aleister
Crowley, Himmler, Garbo and Churchill. Its mood felt, in
that early 1970s way, ominous. I didn't understand it at the
time (I hardly understand it now) but it didn't matter. It
was partly the arrangement of the thing that held me, how
it began as a lonely acoustic lament before bursting out
into operatic thunder, driven by a swirling string score, a
ghost-in-the-mansion piano (Rick Wakeman's) and Bowie's
lovely despairing vocal. I played it all the time, sang along
to it, especially those *ah-ah*, *ah-ah*, *ah-ahs*. That was what
transfixed me – that he sang like he meant it. He did it again
on 'Five Years', another song fit for this plague year, with
his agonised cry of 'five years . . . that's all we've got'.

Bowie became a hero to me in a way that a footballer
never could, because he appealed to a sense of wonder
that wasn't just emotional. His talent touched on something mysterious, something creative, that surpassed

* I was enthralled by the story that Mott were about to split up when
Bowie, an admirer, offered them this song. Of its many wonders I most
love Ian Hunter's monologue over the song's end, apparently addressing
someone in the audience: 'Hey you there . . . in the glasses . . . I want
you . . . I want you at the front . . .' Was he talking to me?

even the spectacle of John Toshack nodding one home in front of the Kop. Football and music weren't exclusive to one another: they were the twin co-ordinates by which I steered my teenage life. Here was the difference. There were a lot of footballers I liked; but Bowie I loved.

Football, music, books, girls. The ordinary passions of a 1970s youth. I came quite late to books. Discovering Graham Greene's *The End of the Affair* pretty much changed my reading life. *Rothmans Football Yearbook* no longer cut it. And as music began to take over I put away childish things like *Shoot!* magazine and began a long and involved relationship with the *NME*. True, it didn't have a weekly column by Kevin Keegan or a Player's Profile, in which you learnt that most footballers' favourite dish was steak and chips. But it did carry lengthy interviews with David Bowie, most of them, it seemed, by Charles Shaar Murray. Those *NME* writers of the late '70s and early '80s – Julie Burchill, Ian Penman, Mark Ellen, Paul Du Noyer, Andy Gill, Paul Morley, Adrian Thrills – were more than bylines to me, they were musical and cultural avatars. I read them every Thursday like holy writ. It's no exaggeration to say that they made me want to be a writer.

It was an *NME* reviewer, or else Barry Norman on *Film 79*, that prompted my fearful 14-year-old self to go and see *The Deer Hunter*, my first ever 'X' film.* From

* For younger readers out there, it's the old version of an '18' – a tame rebranding. An 'X' had a frisson of menace, it represented something dark, possibly unhealthy, definitely verboten.

my mum I had already conceived a love of old black and white movies – I particularly recall watching with her late-night TV screenings of *Arsenic and Old Lace* and *The Man Who Came to Dinner*. But nothing got me like the gut-punch of *The Deer Hunter* – the pale saint's face of Christopher Walken, the horror of Russian roulette, the *wump-wump* of the helicopter gunships – and from that point I was lost to a major celluloid addiction. I studied Classics at university and left in 1986 with a good education – in cinema. Later, I was lucky enough to parlay it into a job as film critic. The *Independent* newspaper had started up the autumn I came to London, and for a few years I wrote book reviews and features for it. At the time I lived in a room so small you had to go outside to change your mind. I didn't earn much and it didn't bother me, because I was doing something I loved. I interviewed writers I revered – Martin Amis, Pauline Kael, E. L. Doctorow, John Updike, Lorrie Moore, Robert Hughes. Were they heroes? I suppose they were.

As an adult the passion for football hadn't dimmed, but it had changed. In the '90s I enjoyed playing it more than watching it – I was involved in a weekend game with old friends, a low-standard affair and a pain to organise, but fun. To be an LFC fan during those years was a frustrating, often distressing experience. We had been comprehensively dethroned by United, and every time a renaissance seemed on the cards it collapsed – another lost illusion. The constitution of a Liverpool side assumed a pattern: it would feature one or two world-class stars, a handful of excellent players, and the remainder honest journeymen. Not bad, but not good enough for LFC. Back in the 1970s and '80s the difference was this: whatever the calibre of player who came through the door at Anfield, his game would invariably be enhanced just by playing for Liverpool. The immemorial greatness of the team's DNA rubbed off on him.

Dalglish's distinction as a manager extended far beyond his run of trophies in the 1980s. His compassion and his willingness to front the collective burden of anguish in the wake of Hillsborough were exemplary. But the responsibility was a heavy one, and his decision to quit in 1991 was plainly a result of exhaustion. The pressure of being in charge at Liverpool is intense at the best of times; Dalglish had known the best and the worst.

The managers who came after him would suffer not just in comparison but often in ways of their own making. Graeme Souness – moustachioed maestro who bestrode the imperial age, part-athlete, part-mob enforcer – took over at a tricky moment. He had inherited an ageing squad and during his time at Rangers had acquired a reputation for intransigence. He was also suffering from a heart condition. After a clear-out he made several ill-advised signings: certain names from that era still make me shudder. All of this might have been survived. His gravest misjudgement was to sell the story of his heart-bypass travails to the *Sun*, anathema to LFC ever since its perpetration of gross falsehoods about fan behaviour at Hillsborough. The paper ran its Souness exclusive on 15 April, the third anniversary of the disaster, compounding the outrage. A natural antagonist, he later apologised for the error, but even at this distance his original decision seems not just deplorable but incomprehensible. It will follow him around.

The joint managership of Roy Evans and Gérard Houllier always looked a doubtful compromise. The closest the English game has ever come to a successful double act was Brian Clough and Peter Taylor, and even that one ended in tears. Evans, a highly regarded lieutenant of the Boot Room, never became the managerial star we'd hoped for. He was also damagingly associated with the 'Spice Boys' folderol. Houllier, LFC's first foreign boss, will always be remembered for his cup Treble of 2000–01, including Michael Owen's late mugging of Arsenal in the FA Cup final at Cardiff. The following year Houllier took Liverpool to a second-place finish behind Arsenal in their Double season. He brought in some quality (Sami Hyypiä, Didi Hamann, Emile Heskey) and personally encouraged the development of the young Steven Gerrard. His misfortune was to be felled by a bolt from the blue: taken ill during a league game versus Leeds at Anfield in October 2001 he suffered a dissected aorta that required an emergency bypass operation. It later emerged that he had escaped death by the narrowest squeak. When he returned to the bench – too early, it was said – he looked gaunt, pale and haunted. It would have been surprising if his confidence had been untroubled; sadly his judgement was shot, too, and he continued the regrettable tradition of Souness and Evans in making some of the worst transfer decisions* in LFC history.

Rafa Benítez steered us to the most improbable of Champions League victories. He made Liverpool a force again in Europe. He signed Fernando Torres and Xabi Alonso. He nearly won us the league in 2008–09, our closest effort in years. And yet I never loved him as our manager. He had the capricious sensibility of an autocrat and a humourless streak as wide as the Mersey. His clash with the owners over transfers revealed a petulant side. When Robbie Keane was signed, apparently over his head, Benítez responded by persistently subbing the player. The board's refusal to sanction the purchase of Gareth Barry from Villa for once made me sympathetic with the board. His 'facts' rant against Ferguson in 2009 wasn't the turning-point in the title race that season, but it was pitiful, and mortifying. Had he learnt nothing from Kevin Keegan? His combative relationship with his employers would eventually usher him towards the exit, though

---

* They included his mishandling of the great Finnish no. 10 Jari Litmanen, who although near the end of a brilliant career still promised much. He had the touch and class of a born Liverpool striker. Houllier, having expressed his delight on signing him from Barcelona ('a world-class player') then chose to ignore him. He eventually moved the player on, with an explanation that defied both logic and common sense: 'I let Jari go because I have always believed he had great potential which could benefit other teams.' Err . . .

seventh place in a mediocre 2009–10 season also suggested we weren't letting go one of the greats.

With the house in uproar under the detested Hicks–Gillett regime it wasn't a happy time for Roy Hodgson to arrive at Anfield. An honourable journeyman and Manager of the Year in 2009–10, he had been more often employed stamping out relegation fires than leading title contenders. The fans sensed this ungainly fit from the start. He seemed at a loss when results went against us, and insisted that spending big in the transfer market wasn't the solution. (Instead he spent small, and badly.) I felt sorry for him, and when a writer friend told me that he'd recently met Hodgson and been impressed by a) his amiability and b) his interest in modern fiction, I decided to send him my first novel. It was called *The Rescue Man*, a title that seemed to chime with the job he was being tasked with at Anfield. Two days later he wrote back, very graciously, thanking me for the book and expressing a hope he might 'enjoy some of the same success as my illustrious predecessors'.

I was chuffed.* Alas, his hope of success at Liverpool was illusory. The sides he put out looked short of cohesion and confidence. We lost too many games. In December bottom-of-the-table Wolves beat us 1–0 at Anfield, and

---

* Years later I met him through an old friend at Crystal Palace and he proved every bit the gentleman I'd imagined. What's more, he'd read my book.

The Liverpool Football Club
& Athletic Grounds Limited
Melwood Training Ground, Deysbrook Lane,
West Derby, Liverpool, L12 8SY
Tel: 0151 282 8888 Fax: 0151 252 2206
www.liverpoolfc.tv

Melwood Training Ground

RH:CT

Mr Anthony Quinn
30 St Paul's Place
London
N1 2QG

26 October 2010

Dear Anthony

I am writing to thank you for sending me a copy of your debut novel "The Rescue Man" which I received today.

I do enjoy reading when I have the time, especially when I can relate to the surroundings in which the story is set.

Thank you for your judicious words of support on my appointment here. I hope I am able to enjoy some of the same success of my illustrious predecessors.

May I wish you all the best for your future as a novelist, and thank you for your continued support of Liverpool Football Club.

Yours sincerely

Roy Hodgson
MANAGER, L.F.C.

Hodgson knew that time was running out. After the game he complained that 'the famous Anfield support has not really been there', a forlorn remark that pretty much sealed his fate. In the first week of January he was gone.

The chaotic nature of Liverpool's transfer dealings dogged Brendan Rodgers's tenure. His energy and ambition at Swansea had impressed Fenway Sports Group, and his relative youth was in notable contrast to the previous incumbents. He was among a new generation of managers happy to talk about analytics and deliver motivational messages – on arriving at Anfield he presented his employers with a 180-page dossier that set out his 'vision'. (Would anyone except on pain of death actually read a 180-page dossier written by a football manager?) Rodgers could certainly talk the talk, and at times I warmed to his appreciation of the club's stature; he understood the privilege of leading Liverpool. Behind the scenes, though, there was many a ding-dong over signings. With Suárez and Sterling both gone in the summer and Sturridge crocked, attacking options were limited. After the bonanza of 101 league goals in 2013–14 the supply faltered – just 52 in 2014–15 – and neither Rickie Lambert nor Balotelli ever looked like making up the shortfall. The club spent £117 million on transfers, yet the manager was still reluctant to field the likes of Emre Can and Jordan Henderson (whom he wanted to sell). In his last interview before being sacked Rodgers spoke of the need for a 'rebuilding' at Anfield that would 'take time'. He was right, but it would be someone else in charge of it.

Football managers don't really cut it as heroes. For one thing, we are not privy to exactly what they do, aside from picking the team. In the Premier League clubs are built upon a hierarchical structure – director of this, head of that – apparently as intricate as the Court of Versailles. When a club is successful it's the players who take most of the kudos. When a club fails it's the manager who carries the can, while someone maybe notes in passing that 'those players should take a long hard look at themselves . . .' We watch the manager – tracksuit pompously monogrammed with his initials – point and shout on the training ground, we listen to him give post-match analyses, we wonder how long he will keep the show on the road. It's only after he's gone that the full story of bust-ups and panic attacks comes out. (I am trying very hard not to think of Graham Taylor recalling his torments as England manager and how he'd wake from a stressful night with 'the pyjamas wet through'.)

Aside from the rare flamboyant oddball – Clough, Malcolm Allison* – managers are mostly a joyless breed. Many wear a permanent expression of affronted dignity, their contempt for 'the media' writ large until they end up

---

* I read Allison's autobiography, *Colours of My Life*, when I was 12, agog. With his fur-collared coat, fedora and a cigar in blast he's the only football manager you could imagine guest-starring in an episode of *The Persuaders*.

redundant and take the broadcasters' shilling themselves. The most notorious exercise a thin frown-line located between paranoia and egomania. They are sulky in defeat and not much perkier in victory. In TV interviews they tend to look like they're being questioned under caution. You could feel for a man who looks so clenched and depressed. But you couldn't warm to him. Managers just aren't *fun*.

Wait, though. Here is an excerpt from my diary, dated 8 October 2015:

> Have been checking the BBC Sport website all week for news, and when it finally arrives I <u>yelp</u> with excitement: Jürgen Klopp has agreed to be manager of Liverpool. Yay! Really like the cut of his jib, he's dry and merry and apparently an inspiration to all who play for him. Jürgen, may you reign long and happily at Anfield! Welcome to Das Boot room.

You may detect a slight tremor of skittishness in my tone. Things get even weirder the next day.

> October 9th 2015: Strange to tell, I've just started dreaming about Jürgen Klopp. R [my wife] says that I have a 'man-crush' on him: she may be right. In the dream I was involved in a training session – <u>of course</u> I'm playing for him – at the end of which I went over to shake his hand (it seemed we hadn't

been properly introduced) and by chance he felt the edge of my sleeve, a cashmere jumper. Why I was wearing cashmere for a footie session wasn't clear, but in any case Klopp smiled and said 'Nice'. Well thanks, Jürgen!

Today he gave his first press conference as LFC manager and was masterly: funny, mischievous, smart, charismatic. 'I am the Normal One', he said, and the press guffawed. Oh please let him be the club's saviour. God knows we've waited long enough for one.

No pressure there, then. Alarming to think Klopp had only been at LFC for 24 hours and already I was dreaming of him. The bounce didn't come instantly. His introduction was a 0–0 draw at White Hart Lane. He got his first Premier League win, 3–1 away to Chelsea – Boom! (my favourite Klopp ebullition) – followed by the deflating 2–1 loss at home to Crystal Palace.

The first evidence of Klopp's signature method came at the Etihad on 21 November. A win for City would put them on top of the table. This is the line-up we fielded that day: Mignolet; Clyne; Škrtel; Lovren; Moreno; Milner; Leiva; Can; Lallana; Firmino; Coutinho. Our usual mixture – two top-class players, a handful on the cusp of good/great, the rest honest toilers. But under Klopp's direction that day they played like world-beaters.

You can pinpoint the very moment it all started, when Coutinho sprints 20 yards across field to dispossess Sagna, carries it towards their box before putting through Firmino. His low cross is spooned into his own net by Mangala. From then on City are caught in a savage storm of *Gegenpressing* and counterattack, which even Gary Neville on Sky calls 'absolutely brilliant from Liverpool', 'scintillating' and later 'the perfect away performance'. Goals from Coutinho and Firmino put us 3–0 up in half an hour, pegged back just before half-time by Agüero. But the storm doesn't abate in the second half and we go 4–1 up with a crashing half-volley from Škrtel.

What had happened? Tactically not much had changed beyond Firmino's being pushed into a central role with support on either side from Lallana and Coutinho. But everything in terms of movement, sharpness and effort felt different. Whatever Klopp had worked on in training had translated directly into performance. This would be the template: motivating his team to play not just to the limit of their capabilities but beyond them.

Take one example: Lucas Leiva had been one of LFC's unglamorous foot-soldiers since signing in 2007. After a difficult early period when the fans got on his back he became a cherished under-the-radar stalwart. Like many defensive midfielders he didn't know how to make a clean tackle and his scoring record was nothing to write home about, literally: one league goal in *ten years*. But under Klopp he somehow became pivotal, deployed either as shield to the back four or as makeshift centre-half when Lovren or Matip was injured. There is a clip of Lucas in one of his last games firing a 30-yarder at goal that squirts harmlessly wide: cut to Klopp on the bench laughing incredulously at the idea of this serial non-scorer trying his luck. But he could afford to laugh knowing he had transformed an ordinary player into a Klopp player.

The win at Man City was a foreglimpse of bright things. If Klopp could exact that kind of performance from a team he had inherited what might he do with players he had actually recruited himself? But it *was* only a foreglimpse. Results in the league during 2015–16 followed a topsy-turvy rhythm, defeats in January to West Ham and Man Utd counterbalanced by an insane 5–4 victory at Norwich where Lallana scored a last-gasp winner and Klopp lost his glasses in the mêlée of celebration. In Europe, however, LFC were carrying all before them, notably in an astonishing game against Klopp's old love Borussia Dortmund. I wrote in my diary:

> April 14th 2016: Another night of barely believable drama at Anfield. After the 1–1 draw at Dortmund there seemed to be a quiet confidence that we would go through, an assumption almost immediately overturned when we went 2–0 down inside nine minutes. It wasn't that Liverpool were bad, just that they were too quick and smart and deadly – both goals came from counterattacks inside Dortmund's

own half. They could have had three or four but for some stout defending. Origi pulled one back for us in the second half, only for them to land a sucker-punch ten minutes later: 3–1. We looked dead and buried . . . except that we weren't, and Coutinho and Sakho dragged us back to 3–3. Into the first minute of extra-time, the crowd roaring them on, Milner floats a lovely cross and Lovren heads home, 4–3. Woo-hoo! It's Saint-Étienne and AC Milan rolled into one. All you need is Lovren – not something I thought I'd ever write.

The odd thing about Klopp's first great European night at Anfield is that it was both scarcely believable and not surprising at all. Liverpool were past masters of the do-or-die occasion, and so was he. It later emerged that his former confreres at Dortmund were upset by Klopp's stirring up of the crowd and his extravagant celebration of the goals, but what did they expect? There was only one way he would ever commit himself to LFC, and that was wholeheartedly.

With our league form floundering a cup would now be the only way to mark Klopp's first season in charge. Having lost the League Cup final to City (on penalties) in February the Europa League became our lifeline, and a 3–0 win over Villarreal in the second-leg semi put us in the final against Sevilla at Basel. We were sitting pretty as we went in at half-time, one-up thanks to Sturridge's exquisitely arrowed outside-of-the-boot finish. Unfortunately our deficiencies were exposed 20 seconds after the restart when a galumphing defensive error by Moreno* let them in to equalise. Sevilla's confidence flooded back and they sank us with two more in 25 minutes; by the end it looked like popguns against battleships. Klopp was philosophical in defeat, though he made his feelings known about certain refereeing decisions – a Lovren header ruled out for offside and their third goal at first disputed but then allowed to stand. 'It is not good to concede a goal straight after half-time but you have 44 minutes to strike back. The reaction was the problem . . . We will use this experience together and then some day everyone will say Basel was a very decisive moment in the future of Liverpool.'

Again, the note of quiet optimism resonates. This was a setback, but also a staging-post on our way back to the top. He would make believers of us yet. In the meantime LFC had ended eighth in the table, between West Ham and Stoke. No European football for us in 2016–17. The boilers at Anfield remained lukewarm.

* A former Sevilla player himself, he would get some flak for this performance – justifiably – and thereafter became more peripheral in the squad. Milner was preferred as a makeshift left-back even when Moreno was fit. Andy Robertson's emergence closed the door on any possibility of a comeback.

7. Mo Better Reds

As a fan you are always waiting for signs, for omens, and the antennae are never more twitchy than on the first day of a new season. In August the combination of sunshine and heat lend an uncertain glare to the occasion. The green of the pitch has tweaked its dazzle up a notch. Are we witnessing that much-heralded dawn (the unfamiliar look of the new kit encourages us) or is it a mirage about to dissolve and plunge us back into the old routine?

The season of 2016–17, Klopp's first full one in charge, began at the Emirates with a seven-goal thriller. It took its time to get going. We were 1–0 down until Coutinho equalised from a brilliant free-kick on the stroke of half-time. After that a switch was flipped and the goals flew in, from Lallana, another from Coutinho, and a blistering solo effort from Mané on his debut. 4–1 up after 63 minutes. Arsenal, briefly shellshocked, pulled a couple back to end the game 4–3. Klopp afterwards berated himself for wildly celebrating the fourth goal with half an hour still to play – 'I knew immediately it was a mistake' – but he looked happy enough in the post-match interview. As he said, if you concede three against Arsenal at the Emirates you generally expect to be on the losing side.

The euphoria was short-lived: the following week we lost 2–0 to Burnley at Turf Moor. Here we go: the rollercoaster again. Klopp had by now instilled the energy and work ethic demanded of his *Gegenpressing* philosophy, and his two big signings of the summer – Mané and Wijnaldum – brought pace and polish to the team. We were beginning to look formidable, especially against the elite: not one of Chelsea, Man Utd, Spurs, Man City or Arsenal managed a league win over us in 2016–17. But while LFC could raise their game at the top, they struggled against teams in the lower echelons, losing to Hull, Swansea, Crystal Palace, Burnley and Bournemouth. This last was especially galling, 3–1 up with 14 minutes to play, we somehow contrived to lose 4–3. Klopp said afterwards, 'We opened the door, but Bournemouth had to run through it – and they did.' Perhaps this disjunction was not so mysterious. Liverpool play much better against sides who favour an expansive game, who push up and leave space for counterattacking. Less gifted sides who defend deep and allow us possession are paradoxically more dangerous, tending to score on the break or from set-pieces – our Achilles heel.

The Bournemouth debacle also brought to an end a 15-game run without defeat. Every time we seemed to be building momentum the car would suddenly stall. In January the wheels almost came off, dumped out of two cups (by Southampton and Plymouth) and facing a record fourth loss on the bounce, against Chelsea: low on confidence we nevertheless squeezed out a 1–1 draw. Klopp refused to be downcast by our spotty form: 'We have to believe in the long-term project. Nobody wants to hear it but losing is a part of football.' Indeed, though losing 2–0 at relegation-threatened Hull probably took the biscuit as low point of the season: baffling as well as humiliating. Klopp admitted, 'We need to wake up; that was not acceptable.'

Form stuttered through the spring as Liverpool joined a pack of teams – United, City, Arsenal – chasing third and fourth place. Chelsea and Tottenham had first and second pretty much in the bag. At the end of April we stepped on another banana skin against Crystal Palace, with Christian Benteke* on his return to Anfield almost inevitably scoring, twice, in their 2–1 win. The final day of the season arrived with LFC desperate for one of two Champions League spots still up for grabs: a win over relegated Middlesbrough at Anfield looked a shoo-in. And of course for 45 minutes it was anything but. We laboured through the gears, lucky not to concede a penalty when Lovren pulled back Bamford. I can recall few goals that brought more relief than Gini Wijnaldum's rifled strike just before the half-time whistle. Then Coutinho and Lallana finished the job in the second half. It was 'tense', as Klopp said, but we had secured fourth spot and a route back to Europe.

---

* What on earth happened to him? Signed in the summer of 2015 he scored some good goals, including our Boxing Day winner against Leicester in their PL-winning season. But LFC no longer required an obvious target man and his game looked ill-matched to Klopp's demands for speed and pressing. Benteke had a maddening habit of playing better at Anfield as an opponent, scoring five times when in Villa or Palace colours. The latter signed him for a fee that now looks like the best offload we ever did.

Interlude: The Clean Team

The Premier League was beyond us, but there was one league LFC did top in 2016–17: the Fair Play League. The team went the whole season without a single player being sent off. We also won it in 2017–18, 2018–19 and 2019–20. (The only LFC player to be sent off last season was Alisson, for handling outside the area against Brighton.) We have also been the cleanest team in Europe. According to the stats Liverpool committed 8.14 fouls per game in 2019–20. This might not be cause to break out the champagne, but it does say something about the way Klopp has developed and refined the style of play he wants. When he arrived at Liverpool amid talk of *Gegenpressing* and 'Heavy Metal Football' the accent on aggression was clearly marked. The tackles were soon flying in, and the team's identity became one of tigerish possession. In the 2015–16 season the team got 58 yellow cards and three red, placing us seventh in the Fair Play League. Don't laugh: Arsenal were top!

Yet something more interesting lies behind the data of fouls and bookings. In an article for *The Times* ('Liverpool the best hunters in history', February 2020) James Gheerbrant considered the question of tackling itself, and how it is often less productive than we think. In 2016–17 Liverpool won possession in the final third 4.34 times a match, the fourth highest in the league. But as they progressed under Klopp the number of tackles actually decreased; until the hiatus in March they made

15.2 tackles per game, the fifth fewest in the league. What they did instead was to close down the space and intercept the ball, thus obviating the risk of a foul or an injury to themselves in a tackle. As Gheerbrant puts it: 'While Klopp has dialled back the collisions, he has sharpened his team's ability to regain the ball where it really matters . . . Last season Liverpool won possession in the final third 4.89 times a match. This season they are doing it 6.62 times, the highest level on record.' In the 1–0 win away at Norwich on 15 February Liverpool regained the ball in the final third 17 times, despite making only 16 tackles in the whole game.

How can this be? One minor factor is that we are no longer compromised by the hopeless lunge-tackling of Moreno or the daintier mistimed trips of Lucas Leiva (I always loved the way after upending someone he would flash that you're-kidding-me smile at the referee). But the larger reason is to do with our tactical press: 'the co-ordinated sequences through which teams win possession high up the pitch and thus avoid the need to make tackles further back'. These tactics have been inculcated and honed at Melwood by Klopp's able lieutenants Peter Krawietz and Pep Lijnders. The latter drills the team in synchronising their movement: 'Wherever we are on the pitch, we are together,' he said.

Most of Liverpool's defensive activity, as Gheerbrant explains, 'takes place level with their opponents' penalty area, or in the band just before it. Almost none occurs in their own box, which is how a team ends up conceding one goal in 11 matches.' When you're that good at anticipating and intercepting the ball you don't need to tackle so much. The best defensive pressure involves giving your opponent no room to move and so forcing him into error. Crowds may not approve the decline of tackling – but it might be the future.

A change came in the 2017–18 season. For all the talk of progress and tactical sophistication there was one thing LFC had lacked for a while: a Torres or a Suárez who could score 20 goals or more per season. In 2016–17 Coutinho was our top scorer with 14, followed by Mané on 13 and Firmino on 12. Not bad, but not sufficient to challenge for a title. In the end it's goals that define a season, goals that keep a manager in his job (or not). As Klopp said, football is quite simple: you shoot the ball in the net.

There was a buzz, of course, attending the arrival of Mohamed Salah from Roma. His record in Italy (29 goals in 65 appearances) was pretty good for a winger, and he hadn't come cheap (£36.5 million plus add-ons). But nobody quite expected the instant and phenomenal effect he would have at Anfield. Slight but sturdy, he was graced with wonderful balance, astonishing close control and a greyhound's turn of speed. One of his most eye-catching skills was his first touch; a ball sent high and swirling 60 yards upfield would seem to drop unerringly onto his boot, as if magnetised. But it was his free scoring that blew us away. He scored (on debut) against Watford on the first day of the season, and he scored against Brighton on the closing day in May. In between he netted another 30 goals in the Premier League and 11 more in Europe. His signature move, cutting in from the right before curling a shot into the far corner with his left, became a thing of beauty. Was this the same player Mourinho bought and then more or less ignored at Chelsea? Not since Decca turned down The Beatles has a talent been so egregiously misread.

In the *Guardian* Barney Ronay wrote a funny and gracious *mea culpa* for initially demurring at a player he now considered 'one of the outstanding bargains of the last ten years'. He went on to wax lyrical in characteristic Ronayan style, identifying 'those moments of out-there physical creativity, the basic joy in his football that bears comparison, even after a single season, to the conjoined Henry-Ronaldo-Suárez-Bergkamp-Agüero attacking godhead of the Premier League years'. By the season's end Salah had won many more admirers, along with the Golden Boot, Premier League Player of the Year, the PFA Player of the Year and the Football Writers' Association Footballer of the Year. There was even a newspaper story that he had had a beneficial effect on religious tolerance in the North West: incidents of aggravation against Muslims were in decline. Mo Better Race Relations!

This new firepower didn't prevent us being spanked 5–0 by City at the Etihad (after Mané was sent off) and 4–1 by Spurs at Wembley (a Lovren horror-show). The usual inconsistency reigned. Some weeks we looked like title contenders; others we were also-rans. Even when we were scoring for fun we leaked goals at the other end – Watford (3–3) in August and Arsenal (3–3) in December. Just before Christmas Philippe Coutinho finally got his transfer to Barça, at a whopping £142 million – money too crazy to turn down. Klopp had spoken of 'Phil' throughout as if he were a cherished son, but he knew there was no keeping a player so determined to make a move. He had been through tearful partings with young stars like Götze and Kagawa at Dortmund, but this time there was no histrionic talk of heart-attacks or nights out ruined. He had learnt acceptance.

Coutinho *had* been wonderful for us. As well as 54 goals and numerous assists in his 201 league and cup appearances he had also been the team's tireless dynamo of invention. During his time in the Premier League his only rivals as playmaker were David Silva and Eden Hazard.

But when one door closes . . . The loss of Coutinho wasn't as grievous as it might have been now that our attacking triumvirate of Mané, Firmino and Salah were firing on all cylinders. And the money Barcelona paid out was immediately turned to advantage by the longed-for acquisition of Virgil van Dijk in January 2018. In fact we were having a fair season, fourth in the table at Christmas on 34 points. Too bad we were a mere 18 behind leaders City, who were destroying all in their path and breaking a load of Premier League records to boot. They were still unbeaten when they came to Anfield on 14 January, the first, as it turned out, of three epic encounters before the season's end. When Salah lifted the ball 40 yards into the net from Ederson's shanked clearance we were 4–1 up on 68 minutes. After a tight first half this might have been a rout, had City not then remembered they were champions elect and pulled back two late goals to make it 4–3.

We would play them twice again in April in the quarter-finals of the Champions League. At Anfield we blitzed them in a 20-minute period with goals from Salah, Oxlade-Chamberlain (a belter) and Mané, seeming to guarantee a passage to the semis. The return leg at the Etihad immediately called for battle stations as Gabriel Jesus scored inside two minutes and City put us on 'the carousel'. They nearly passed us to death in the first half and should have gone in 2–0 up but for Sané's bundled goal being (mistakenly) disallowed. Bernardo Silva fizzed a shot against the post. Their domination felt like revenge for the spell we had cast on them at Anfield. But the storm blew itself out in the second half. Guardiola, sent to the stands for his furious reaction to the disallowed goal, could only watch as Liverpool came off the ropes and equalised through Salah's deft chip. Firmino coolly added another late on and put the tie beyond reach. In this, a monumental test of nerve and concentration, we had stood firm against the best team in the Premier League and restricted them to a single goal. For Klopp it was also a personal triumph, being the seventh time he had beaten a Guardiola team, more than any other manager.

There were quite a few to pick from, of course, but the home leg semi against Roma was maybe Salah's game of the season. Roma started brightly, hitting the bar when Karius flapped at Kolarov's drive (a grim foreshadowing of his mistake with Bale's second goal in Kiev), but the high defensive line they set looked hugely risky. Hadn't they bothered to watch us play this season? On 35 minutes Salah, finding space on the edge of the area, cut inside and curled in a beauty off the underside of the bar. He made it 2–0 just before half-time, dinking the ball over the advancing keeper (Alisson, poor feller!) after Firmino's delicate prod through. Salah didn't celebrate either of the goals out of respect for his old club, but most of Anfield did, riotously. In the second half he created – right foot this time – a goal each for Mané and Firmino, who added another with a free header. Only the second time in a CL semi that a team had scored five goals.* It was such a complete display that even Roma's two late goals felt like consolation prizes – *Crackerjack* pencils for showing up. They also scored a couple of late goals in the return leg in Rome, winning 4–2, but again it was too little, too late. LFC were in a Champions League final for the first time in 11 years.

Which we lost 3–1 in Kiev. But let's not dwell.

City had won the title at a majestic stroll with 100 points, 19 ahead of United in second and 25 ahead of Liverpool

---

* The first time was Ajax in 1995, 5–2 against Bayern Munich.

in fourth. Even I could do the maths on this one: if we wanted to get anywhere near City next season we would have to improve our game by 25 per cent. Considered in those terms it didn't look possible. The team had played outstandingly in 2017–18, we had beaten the champions three times, we had scored 84 goals in the league and a record 47 goals[*] in 15 Champions League games. And yet we had ended up with zilch.

[*] Barcelona were the previous record holders, 45 goals in 16 games during 1999–2000.

8. Fußball, Bloody Hell

'If you're first you're first, if you're second you're nothing,' said Shankly. Did that judgement prey on the minds of Liverpool fans as the team continued its high-wire act atop the Premier League table in December 2018? I can't say that it preyed on mine; I was too absorbed in the *Sturm und Drang* of our week-by-week refusal to be beaten. We had so far won 17 out of 20 league games, scoring 40 goals. Even a couple of the games we had drawn felt like victories: a last-minute equaliser against Chelsea at the Bridge will be remembered as the greatest goal Daniel Sturridge ever scored for us, while we might have gone down to City at Anfield had Mahrez not blazed their late penalty over the bar. The signs pointed to our luck being in, never more so than when Div nodded in his Big Derby Goal on 96 minutes. (Still wondering about that assist.) We ended the year with a majestic 5–1 drubbing of Arsenal, a game I watched in the pub at the end of our road. I *yelped* when Bobby Firmino (hat-trick hero) slalomed through their defence to slot his second. I recall a few heads turning: you're never far from a Gooner where I live.

So we were top on 54 points, nine ahead of Spurs in second, ten ahead of City in third. Leaders at Christmas, as everyone knows, go on to win the title, bar two exceptions in the last ten years, 2008–09 and 2013–14. And who lost it then? Klopp in any case would not countenance talk of titles, and no wonder; he knew better than most from his time at Mainz about being pipped at the post. When you're a coach you don't just manage a team, you manage expectations too. Still, 'in 2018 I have nothing to moan about,' he said. The side looked better balanced, with Trent Alexander-Arnold and Andy Robertson fast becoming our most dangerous threat from the wings, Henderson, Fabinho and Wijnaldum the molten steel in the middle, and our front three the wild mercury. The signal change from last season was our defensive assurance, overseen by Virgil and his lieutenants, Matip, Gomez or Lovren. And we could all heave a sigh of relief knowing Alisson was betwixt the sticks.

Our first game of 2019 was already looking to be the pivotal fixture of the season. City knew it was a must-win at the Etihad on 3 January, and the tension on either side lent a frenetic rhythm to the game. Klopp complained that Kompany's last-man challenge on Salah ought to have been punished with a red card, though it didn't look clear-cut. In the end it came down to a matter of millimetres when, on 18 minutes, Mané's shot rebounded off the post against Ederson and rolled agonisingly onto the line: Stones scooped away the ball before it crossed. Saved by the length of a gnat's eyebrow. Agüero eventually opened the scoring, from an impossible angle, just before half-time. It looked like we'd got a point after Firmino equalised with a header, only for Sané to rifle a shot across

Alisson that hit the post (the same one as Mané had) and this time went in off. Fine margins . . . Could we have guessed then just how fine?

You could argue that we lost the league that night, though it's perhaps more instructive to consider the draws in February and March that clogged our progress, against Leicester, West Ham (both 1–1), Man Utd and Everton (both 0–0). My diary entry:

> March 3rd, 2019: To Tom's,* on a blustery wet afternoon, for the Everton–Liverpool game at Goodison. We have the best chances – a Salah one-on-one with Pickford, a second-half scramble that Fabinho should have put away – but it ends 0–0 and inevitably cranks up the talk of Liverpool 'bottling it'. We've not conceded a goal in five games, we're a single point behind Man City, we've lost one match all season – and yet the reports will all talk about L'pool 'losing their way'. Klopp blamed the wind, probably not helpful but it's the same for both teams.

---

* My best friend, with whom I have watched so much footie. A Spurs fan, poor chap. The only time we have ever fallen out was at dinner in an Islington steak-house circa 1998. The argument concerned whether Kevin Keegan (see under 'K', in the ShanKlopp A–Z) was 'an idiot' or not. I don't recall who won but Tom got so angry that he did something I've only ever seen happen in bad television – threw his half of the bill on the table before storming out. I would love to see his face reading this now – *love it*.

I detect nerves in there. That's what comes of reading the match reports *and* all the message-boards. There are times when you want to attain a Klopp-like calm and cut out distractions, but it's hard to shake that quest for favourable omens – for reassurance. I kept searching for articles that would explain why City couldn't possibly hold on to their one-point lead till the end. And once I'd read them I would try to convince myself they were right.

In the meantime we had taken a helter-skelter ride on the Champions League circuit, managing to get our worst performance of the season – a 2–0 defeat to Red Star Belgrade in November – quickly out of the system. (Asked if he could put his finger on what went wrong Klopp replied, 'I only have ten fingers.') In March, ten days after that miserable draw at Goodison, we gave what was up till then our best performance of the season in the first knock-out round at the Allianz Arena. Bayern had held us 0–0 at Anfield in the first leg and must have fancied themselves, but Klopp, versed in the wiles of the Munich Death Star, had primed the team expertly. They closed and pressed and harried Bayern out of their stride, and even losing Henderson early on wasn't the disruption we feared. Despite their formidable attacking options – Ribéry, Lewandowski, James Rodríguez, Gnabry – Bayern looked short of ideas. Mané's superb opener from Virge's long ball – the touch and swivel before lifting it sweetly into the far corner – gave notice that LFC were in the form of their lives. Even when they equalised via

Matip's unlucky own goal we looked rock-steady; a towering header from Virge and another from Mané courtesy of Salah's wonderful cross eased us into the quarters.

Where we dismissed Porto with almost imperious cool, 2–0 at Anfield and 4–1 at their place. But wait, who was that heading towards us in the semis? Only Barcelona. True, it wasn't the Barcelona of Pep's golden age, the team of Iniesta and Xavi, the team you could barely get the ball off, but still – it was Barcelona, led by the best player in the world. Messi in fact played a decisive role at the Nou Camp, where we might have escaped with only a 1–0 deficit (Suárez's first-half strike) had not Barça's talisman delivered a crushing double-blow in the last 15 minutes. First, he tapped in a rebound off the bar. Then he bent a free-kick from 30 yards into the top corner, a strike so perfectly placed that not even spring-heeled Alisson – all 6ft 3 of him – could get near it.* Klopp tipped his hat to the 'unstoppable' Messi afterwards, though he believed Liverpool had controlled the game in the second half. 'I told the boys I'm proud of how we played. Against a side like this . . . I was completely happy.' He also rued the chances we missed, in particular Salah hitting the post from three yards out. 'Football is like this. It's about scoring goals – they scored three and we scored none.' It might have ended worse for us if Dembélé had put away a sitter in the dying seconds.

* His 600th goal for Barcelona, 14 years to the day since he had scored his first.

Do you remember how you felt around 7.30 p.m. on 7 May 2019, as you were settling down for the second leg of the semi? I watched it in a pub in Bloomsbury with my younger brother and a mate, same as we had done all season, each of us excited but sharing a sense of resignation about the evening: much as we wished it otherwise there was no use kidding ourselves. Barça were too good to let a 3–0 lead slip, and too chastened by the horror of 2018 – when Roma overhauled a 4–1 deficit to dump them out of the CL quarter-final – to make the same mistake again. Some 'Pool fans will insist they 'always knew' we could do it, but even the wild optimists of my acquaintance didn't really fancy our chances. Oh, but that gladiatorial roar of Anfield as the teams walked out did make us wonder . . .

'History or heartbreak, it's do or die for Liverpool,' announced Darren Fletcher on BT Sport, an absurdly grandiose start (and a phrase that screams 'here's one I prepared earlier') though his commentary thereafter met the mood of the occasion: he had a good game.* So too did his sidekick Steve McManaman, whose bumptiousness and wise-after-the-event pontifications usually grate on my ear; this evening he too got the tone right.

The team news was lowering, with both Firmino and Salah *hors de combat*. Divock Origi, who had scored a

---

* A year on the game's highlights have been watched over 12 million times, half of them by me.

late, late winner against Newcastle at the weekend, is a diligent workhorse but hardly in the class of his injured colleagues. I hadn't much faith in him getting the better of a defence like Barcelona's. Ha! O ye of little faith. Div notched our first on seven minutes with a tap-in after ter Stegen only palmed away Henderson's shot, and from that moment the delirium level began to climb steadily. When Robertson impudently ruffled Messi's hair following a challenge I had a moment of panic – the lad is too pumped, he'll get himself sent off. Messi's expression looked like someone had just dropped a cherry bomb in his sangria.

Let no one imagine that Barça 'froze' here. On the night they had the lion's share of possession (57–43 per cent) and even below par they always looked capable of sneaking back into the game. In the first half especially Alisson had to be at his most agile, keeping out a rasping Messi drive, another from Coutinho and a Jordi Alba one-on-one from Messi's brilliant threaded pass. As we kept being reminded, they needed only a single goal that would then oblige us to score five. Messi looked capable of it, if none of his teammates did, and the heart skipped a beat in the early minutes of the second half when he put through Suárez. Ordinarily you would have backed him to finish it, but perhaps even he was overawed by the occasion as he shot weakly against Allison. Suárez, booed all night by the fans, had already supplied an inadvertent helping hand, in any case; his foul had forced Klopp to sub Robertson at half-time and replace him with Gini Wijnaldum . . .

There's often talk around a game like this that one side 'wanted it more'. I'm not sure that Barcelona wanted it any less than we did; the difference was that we were playing like we *needed* it more. We looked that bit sharper, quicker than they did: Klopp had lit the fire in his 'boys'. On 54 minutes, deep inside their half, Trent Alexander-Arnold directed a feeble header at Rakitić, who steered the ball left. But instead of retreating Alexander-Arnold immediately won possession back off Alba – here was *Gegenpressing* encapsulated – and fired in a low cross that Wijnaldum, arriving on the run, connected with firmly. Ter Stegen got a hand to the ball which, delightfully, cannoned in off his back. 2–0. Two minutes later Shaqiri, ineffectual up to now, received the ball on the left from Milner and curled in a sumptuous cross that Wijnaldum – truly, the man of the moment – headed past a stationary ter Stegen. ('Wijnaldum – OH IT'S THREE! LIVERPOOL ARE ALL THE WAY BACK!' cried Fletch. And watching on the replay, 'Barcelona don't fancy it, *do they*?' asked Macca, not sure if the question was rhetorical.) It was true. Barcelona, flakier than a millefeuille in a high wind, looked to be on the verge of collapse. Whenever the camera focused on Coutinho looking disconsolate I thought, 'Oh Phil, you really backed the wrong horse this time.'

We could feel another one coming, maybe in extra time. But no one could have predicted the way it came, because no one had seen anything like it before. I have watched our fourth goal so often now that I ought to be sick of it, yet the beautiful nerve, the unworldly *cheek* of it, gets me every time. Awarded a corner Trent has placed the ball and is ambling away when he stops, sees Origi lurking on the edge of their six-yard box and almost in one movement steps back and drills the ball hard towards him. Now it's one thing to spot a Barcelona defence napping; it's quite another to find your teammate, on the spur of the moment, with pinpoint accuracy. Div also has to adjust his body as the ball arrives at a fast skim, and sidefoots it on the bounce into the top bin. And then he does one other great thing: unlike most other strikers Div doesn't sprint off to celebrate, he *lopes* off, wagging a nonchalant finger, as if to say, 'Yeah, I scored, so what?'

So, pandemonium. It later emerged that Klopp had missed the moment himself, his back to the goal when it happened, but even those of us who were watching could hardly take it in.* When the final whistle came, and the crowd's roar with it, some of the players fell to their knees in tears. Mo Salah, wearing a T-shirt emblazoned with 'NEVER GIVE UP', had the broadest smile in the stadium.

At the press conference the manager looked quietly stunned by his team's achievement. 'If I have to describe this club it's a big heart and tonight it was pounding like crazy,' Klopp said. This was the moment he described his

---

* In the *Guardian* comments section one correspondent spoke for many: 'As I watched it I shouted "what?!" at my TV despite being the only person in the room . . . in all my years of fandom I don't believe I've ever seen a quick corner into the box, and with such success, on such a stage, with such decisive importance.'

players as 'mentality giants', having matched City toe-to-toe all season, having lost to Barcelona the previous week, having faced them this evening without two key players. 'I said to the boys before, "I don't think it's possible but because it's you I think we have a chance" – it's unbelievable.' In the days following, as the astonishments of the game were sinking in, I couldn't stop thinking about that fourth goal. Not to take away anything from Trent himself, but it occurred to me that his brilliant inspiration partly belonged to Klopp – who had promoted him as a teenager, backed him as a first-team player and, crucially, instilled in him the confidence to try something as audacious as that. To accept the risk of looking silly if it didn't come off. The skill, the quick thinking was all Trent's. But the groundwork was all Klopp's.

The instant mythology that sprang up after the game also prompted a debate as to whether this was the greatest comeback in Champions League history, better even than Istanbul in 2005. (Spurs fans may argue that the greatest was actually their own semi-final miracle against Ajax a mere 24 hours after we beat Barcelona.) Purely as a result the 3–3 against Milan feels more unlikely; indeed when you consider it today it seems inexplicable. This was the LFC team that evening: Dudek; Finnan (Hamann h-t); Carragher; Hyypiä; Traoré; Luis García; Gerrard; Alonso; Riise; Kewell (Šmicer 23); Baroš (Cissé 85). Some decent players in there, the sort generally defined as 'great servants of the club'; plus two world-class players in Gerrard and Alonso. Now look at the Milan line-up: Dida; Cafu; Nesta; Stam; Maldini; Pirlo; Gattuso (Rui Costa 111); Seedorf (Serginho 85); Kaká; Shevchenko; Crespo (Tomasson 85). How on earth did we beat a team that had Pirlo, Maldini, Nesta, Kaká and Crespo – big chiefs among the braves – in it? Well, by a will to win, resilience, luck – and inspirational goalkeeping from Jerzy Dudek. And we only beat them on penalties, lest we forget.

The Liverpool side that beat Barça hadn't a weak link in it. We had already matched them at the Nou Camp and lost. At Anfield we outfought and outplayed them, man for man. So the difference to me between our fifth and our sixth Champions League victories is this. Of 2005 I still think, 'How did that happen?' Of 2019 I think, 'We deserved it completely.' The one downside of the final in Madrid was its air of anti-climax. There was just no more drama to go round after those two epic semis, and, *pace* Spurs and their fans, the force of destiny was all with Liverpool. It felt more like a coronation than a contest. A dodgy penalty after two minutes put the game in a dull stranglehold from which neither side really broke free. Allison made a couple of good saves before Div – who else? – clinched it with a fine low drive minutes before the end.

More enjoyable than almost anything that happened in the game is a six-minute film on YouTube, *Jürgen Klopp's Madrid Celebrations Uncut*, in which the camera simply tracks Klopp in the immediate aftermath of the final whistle. No commentary is supplied, and none is needed, as we watch him embrace each of the players, the staff, a few of the Tottenham lads. There's no air-punching or fist-shaking, just a solo, slightly dazed wander about the pitch as euphoria breaks out around him. If it doesn't put a smile on your face, nothing will.

Oh, and City had won the 2018–19 title. By a point.

9. Look Ma, No Fans

29 May 2020. It tells you something about how quickly times can change that until March this year the major controversy in football surrounded the use and misuse of VAR. In the wake of what has happened since, VAR now looks about as relevant as Nigel Farage, or a third runway at Heathrow – those dinosaurs. A global pandemic has that effect.* Daily death tolls have eclipsed other concerns for a while. The social and economic changes being wrought by coronavirus are seismic, and will reverberate for years. Jobs and livelihoods will be lost.

But life doesn't stop, even when a lockdown makes it appear to, and football has come back blinking into the daylight. The Bundesliga, which resumed matches on 16 May, was the heroic canary in the coalmine. Trust the Germans to kick off again. Clips broadcast so far of what they call 'ghost games' convey an atmosphere of eeriness tinged with melancholy. The echoing shouts of a training session come to mind, and the synthetic rasp of the ball hitting the net sounds like a shower curtain whipped back smartly on its rod. It's football, Jim, but not as we know it. Klopp, interviewed on BBC's *Football Focus*, put

* No. 1 song on my Lockdown Playlist: 'Nothing That Has Happened So Far Has Been Anything We Could Control' by Tame Impala. Wordy but prescient.

the best possible spin on the closed-doors policy: 'We all started playing football without supporters and we loved this game not because of the atmosphere in a stadium.' True enough. The five-a-side game I've been playing in Clerkenwell for the last 17 years has never attracted so much as a single supporter, and yet *the quality* on show . . .

Other countries will follow Germany's lead. After long dithering over 'Project Restart', the Premier League yesterday announced that it would recommence on 17 June. Two cheers for that. As well as games played in empty stadiums, social distancing will be observed among the players. Neutral venues have been mooted for certain key matches to keep the crowds away. And there remains the possibility of another cancellation if a second wave of the virus takes hold. The interruption has given us plenty of time to wonder, and to worry. It seems a long time ago that we beat Bournemouth 2–1 at Anfield on 7 March. The next day United beat City 2–0 at Old Trafford, leaving LFC two victories away from our first league title in 30 years. 82 points from 29 games, an incredible 25 points ahead of City in second place. Basically we could have donated our remaining nine games to charity and still won the Premier League by a street. Instead we've been stuck, trapped in the elevator, two floors away from our destination.

Rather than bemoaning our misfortune, perhaps we should rejoice in what the team has already achieved in 2019–20. Purely in terms of statistics this will probably be Liverpool's greatest league season. If the club manages to add 19 more points from the remaining nine games we will overhaul City's record of 100 from two years ago. It would also exceed our own of 97 points in a season from last year. The win against Bournemouth was our 22nd on the run at home, beating Shankly's record of 21 from January to December 1972. But greatness as we know doesn't lie only in numbers. The peculiar aspect of this season is that we haven't always played brilliantly – certainly not to the standard of 2018–19 – and yet we have mastered the irresistible habit of winning. This might reflect on a decline in the quality of Premier League opposition, though it's also to do with that nebulous word 'character'. After a hard-fought 2–1 victory over Chelsea at Stamford Bridge in September Klopp marvelled at his players: 'I shouldn't be surprised about the character of my team any more. Without character life is difficult but football is impossible.' Here's a diary extract from 23 November, when I saw them at Selhurst Park:

> . . . We go in 0–0 at half-time having escaped with a VAR – Palace had a goal chalked off for a foul on Lovren. Second half Mané bags one for us and we seem to be closing the game out when Zaha equalises. Aagh! Two minutes later we're back in front after Bobby Firmino clips in a loose ball from short range: 2–1. Out of jail, and another three points, though we really didn't play well. It's an

oddity of this campaign that we're playing much less fluently than a year ago yet we keep on winning.

Is this 'character'? We've struggled in almost every game I've watched this season, and yet there we are, eight points ahead at the top. We might just grind our way to the title at this rate.

Our season opener, beating Norwich 4–1, was somewhat clouded by the loss of Alisson, who sustained a calf injury that would keep him out till November. Adrián deputised for him superbly, in the league at least. For 2019–20 we sported a kit whose white pinstripe and gold liver bird crest was a throwback to the shirt LFC wore during the all-conquering phase of 1983–85 (Umbro plus Crown Paints). An omen right there.

On Christmas Day we were top, again, having won every league match bar one – a 1–1 draw at Old Trafford in October, also nicked in the final minutes when Lallana equalised for us. A 3–1 victory over City at Anfield in November felt like a tilt in the balance of power. Fabinho's booming 25-yard strike on six minutes set us up for the afternoon. On Boxing Day we went to Leicester, who lay in second. I felt unaccountably nervous about this fixture, even with a ten-point cushion. There had only been four days to recover from the trip to Qatar for the Club World Cup, and Leicester were playing their best football since the 2015–16 title season. As it turned out the mentality monsters were ready for it. A Firmino header from Alexander-Arnold's superb cross had put us 1–0 at half-time without Leicester having mustered a single shot on target. In the second half we put a hatful of missed chances behind us and completely overwhelmed them, first with a Milner penalty, then a cool close finish from Firmino, and finally a beautiful angled drive from Alexander-Arnold, running onto Mané's pass. It was reminiscent of Carlos Alberto's immortal finish* in Brazil's 1970 World Cup win over Italy – also a fourth goal, also by one of the great full-backs.

The 13-point lead we now had was the biggest Boxing Day margin since United's in 1993–94. Klopp was quick to voice his caution. 'We don't feel it, we don't think about it,' he said. 'I can write the stories by myself. Never before in the history of British football has a team had a bigger lead and lost the lead. That sounds negative in my head and we are just focused on the next games.'

The harder you practise, the luckier you get, so the saying goes. But Liverpool's luck sometimes came as a gift from heaven. It was impossible to ignore, for instance, how often opponents missed sitters at vital moments during our long winning run. At Anfield against bottom-of-the-table Watford in December we could have been two goals down had they taken their chances: first Doucouré horribly mistimed a shot when invitingly placed, then Sarr, sizing up a juicy rebound inside the box shinned it comically. Hanging on 1–0 against Tottenham in January they

---

* An immaculate finish, too – note how the ball from Pelé bobbled just before Alberto struck it.

fluffed two late chances – one by Son, the other Lo Celso – that might have turned the game upside down. A few days later at Anfield leading Utd 1–0 Martial burst into our penalty area, one-on-one with Alisson – and skied it. Maybe you could ascribe this profligate finishing to our aura of invincibility: opponents suddenly finding themselves 'with only the goalkeeper to beat' seemed spooked by the chance of glory and panicked.

Twenty-seven league games, 26 won, one drawn. The idea of matching Arsenal's 'Invincibles' had been in the air for a while. Our dominance was unarguable, but could our luck hold too? On the last weekend of February I got the train from Euston to Liverpool with my younger brother. I hadn't been back to Liverpool since my dad died a year ago and we had arranged with my sister and older brother to mark his anniversary with dinner in town. We found the city centre in a carnival mood:

February 29th 2020: Mathew Street on a Saturday afternoon is like a vision of Hogarth, gangs of blokes and hen parties swarming about, people in and out of pubs, a couple of which are blasting out music at nightclub decibels. Pete and I are looking for a pub to watch the Liverpool game but everywhere is rammed, even the pubs (e.g. The Grapes) without TV. Eventually we stop at one I remember from years ago, The Slaughterhouse, which had sawdust on the floor last time I was there. The place now

heaving with people: the drinking here is prodigious!
By a miracle we manage to nab a spec and settle in
front of the screen for Watford–Liverpool . . . and
we crash 3–0. To Watford! Who deserved it by the
way, and could have had four by the end. We were
desperately poor, no rhythm, no snap in attack, and
crucially, I think, no Henderson. He's just the man
to drive on the team when we need it; God knows
what he made of the performance, looking on from
the bench. I get chatting to a young bloke, Jake
Doran, who's a wedding singer with a weekend gig
at the pub. Earns £1,000 per wedding – 'I used to be
one gig away from sleeping on the streets,' he told
me with a laugh. He was friendly, and so was his
mate, a skinny punkish feller who looked like he was
in a band, too . . .

Watford 3–LFC 0. How did it feel? Like a wild party
coming to the boil when a whisper goes round that the
host has just dropped dead. Nobody can quite believe it
– but we're in Liverpool, so everyone keeps on drinking.
Defeat at Watford marked the end of an unbeaten run of
44 games that started in January 2019. Arsenal's run of 49
remains the Premier League record.

Something else was coming to an end that day – an era,
no less. The idea of a pub being rammed belongs to 2020
BC (Before Coronavirus). And we now live in 2020 AD
(Age of Disease).

21 June 2020. So we were back, following the strangest, saddest hiatus in post-war football. LFC's first fixture of the restart was against Everton, one of the games the PL had tentatively scheduled at a neutral venue for fear of crowds gathering outside the stadium. But once Merseyside Police sanctioned it and safety measures were confirmed Goodison got the nod.

Not that you'd have known it was Goodison, or any other famous ground come to that. If the empty terraces looked strange to us watching at home it must have felt a hundredfold stranger to those players walking out into the applauseless air. I honestly felt sorry for them; they didn't look raring to go, they looked a bit lost, bemused by the stillness and the silence. Klopp seemed livelier, sharing a joke with Ancelotti before kick-off, but he knew the challenge awaiting in this new reality. In his pre-match remarks he had not only questioned the British government's dozy response to the pandemic – why so late with the face masks? – he had also suggested that this Premier League season might now be the toughest to win, and that an asterisk, far from demeaning the achievement, would burnish it. (He admitted that he had had to consult a dictionary for the meaning of 'asterisk'.)

With the title a formality, the question now was whether Liverpool could finish the job in a style that matched the first half of our season. And the answer at the conclusion of this, the 236th derby, was an enormous 'uh'. Leaving aside the weird acoustics that picked up the players' voices, the game quickly developed into a hectic anti-climax, Everton set up by Ancelotti to defend deep and look for the counterattack, Liverpool's expansive press-and-pass tactics stymied by a rusty rhythm and the absence of Salah and Robertson.

Our passing, usually so crisp, was off the beam. Tackles flew in, as they always do in a derby, but neither side could get any purchase on the game. It was fierce, it was tight, it was (face it) dreary as hell. Only in the last ten minutes, when Lovren replaced the injured Matip, did Everton scent a whiff of blood. From a Richarlison cross Calvert-Lewin conjured a clever flick that Alisson palmed away; Davies, following up, angled a shot that brushed Joe Gomez before clipping the post. It was close, but we'd escaped with a point.

The first game back at Anfield would be another test. Would the absence of home support spook the players? It also felt slightly ominous that our opponents were Crystal Palace, who had in recent years assumed the aura of a bogey team. Their visit to Anfield in November 2015 marked Klopp's first defeat and his public expression of unhappiness at the sight of fans streaming for the exits before the final whistle.* They were also the last team to win at Anfield in the league, back in April 2017, as my Palace mate

* This is the fourth time I have mentioned this game in these pages. I swear it will be the last.

Stephen reminded me as we settled down in his living room to watch this evening's game. Anfield, empty though it was, had dressed for the occasion with flags and banners draping the stands, a salute to the absent thousands.

The signs were there . . . and the signs meant zip as Liverpool graced the night with their most incisive and imperious game since Leicester at Christmas. Palace, unlucky to lose Zaha after 15 minutes with a muscle strain, couldn't find a way through our relentless press and fell back, raggedly raising a blockade. Lining up a free-kick a few yards outside their box Alexander-Arnold, whose crossing had been woeful against Everton, curled the ball magnificently into the top bin. On the touchline Klopp clenched a fist in triumph. Just before half-time Fabinho, in complete control of the midfield, lifted a sweet pass over their full-back into the path of Salah, who took it on his chest before steering home. The high-tempo vibrancy continued into the second half, Fabinho crowning a man-of-the-match performance with a peachy strike from 30 yards that arrowed past Hennessey. 3–0 became 4–0 as Firmino, Salah and Mané combined in one of those glorious geometrical moves that Mané finished off with Palace defenders trailing in his wake. It was a measure of Liverpool's mastery that Palace failed to have a single touch in our penalty area, a unique and unwanted Premier League record.

Klopp paid tribute to his team afterwards, marvelling at their commitment and hunger even inside a sterile environment: 'We showed our supporters the respect they deserve – that we can play like they are here even when they are not here. Yes, they can push us to incredible things and I never missed them more than tonight – imagine if this game had happened with 55,000 people in the stadium.' The team's performance was, in the words of one reporter, 'virtuosity in a vacuum'.

Being the guest of a Palace shareholder on the night I tried to compensate for my inner glow by reminding Stephen that at least it wasn't the 9–0 humiliation we visited on them back in 1989. 'I was at that game,' he said, 'and we were better then than we were tonight – we had several chances and missed a penalty.'

That 9–0 victory was a famous stop on LFC's procession to the 1989–90 league title, the last time (in case anyone needed reminding) we won it. My God, I was 26 the last time we were champions, the summer of Italia '90, Gazza's tears and the goal-rush of Totò Schillaci. Alan Hansen lifting the trophy back then was no strange sight to us. I suppose I ought to have prepared a little in advance of our 2020 title, but I still had a feeling (a hope) we might win it at the Etihad in July. I had the silly idea of getting a bottle of 1990 Pol Roger to toast the moment, until I checked the price on Wine-Searcher (£200). I decided Louis Roederer NV (£27) would do fine. So there I was on the sofa, following the Chelsea–Man City game on the BBC website, unsure if a result handed to us by City would be as satisfying as a win out on the field. But 'out on the field' didn't mean the same now anyway, not in a near-vacant ground with 300 people in face masks. By the time Willian had put Chelsea 2–1 up I popped the champagne, our title win headlining the BBC 10 o'clock news and my inbox filling up with messages from friends. After 30 years of hurt it wasn't the all-singing, all-dancing *olé-olé-olé* I'd envisaged. But it felt all right.

Klopp himself, fighting back tears, spoke from the team hotel in Formby. 'We had to convince people and that is what we did together. It is a big moment. I am completely overwhelmed. I had no idea it would feel like this.'* He dedicated the win to the fans. 'It is for you. It is incredible. I could not be more proud. Celebrate it at home or in front of your house.' Thousands of them were already going nuts outside Anfield in a swirling fog of red flares. He spoke of the achievement of his players, of the 'huge joy' it was to coach them and the 'consistency' that had driven them. Arrayed across the Sky screen was a trio of Anfield greats – Souness, Dalglish, Phil Thompson – to offer him congratulations, but eventually the emotion cut too deep and Klopp chokingly excused himself ('All the best') and exited the shot. I wish I'd cried too, but I didn't. The feeling that overwhelmed me was relief. Happiness would come later.

So we had the title at last – Hey 19! – and our very first in the Premier League. We had won it with seven games to

---

* Klopp is also a hat-trick hero, being only the third manager, after Guardiola and Ancelotti, to have won the Premier League, the Bundesliga and the Champions League.

spare, a record previously shared by City and United with five. We were back on the perch from which Ferguson and United had crowingly ejected us in the 1990s. My favourite message was a handwritten note from Barry, our milkman, Hackney-born and bred but an LFC fan from boyhood after watching Liverpool play Arsenal on the first ever *Match of the Day* in August 1964: 'Well we done it mate, about time but let's hope it's the start of things to come. YNWA.'

Of all our players the one I felt most chuffed for was Jordan Henderson, living proof that a team's Most Valuable Player is not necessarily your best player, or even your sixth best. He had endured plenty of brickbats in his time, famously from Ferguson, who highlighted a flaw in the player's inclination to 'run from his knees', whereas the modern footballer runs from his hips. (I recall Henderson being informed of this criticism on TV and his extraordinarily polite refusal to rise to the bait.) And yet a fair bit of the flak came from Liverpool fans, carping at his slowness, his safety-first pass back, his inability – noted by Barney Ronay, among others – to take the ball on the half-turn. His presence in the team has provoked amazing levels of hostility.

Strength of character got him through. It seems unarguable that every great side needs a player like Henderson. Of past legends he most reminds me of Bryan Robson, the original Captain Fantastic, the dynamo who by sheer gumption could drag a team to the summit. The sort of player who would rather pluck his own eyes out than be accused of 'giving less than 100 per cent'. When Rodgers tried to offload him to Fulham in 2012 Henderson turned down the move, preferring to fight for his place in the team. It was a decisive moment. Klopp's arrival at Anfield rejuvenated him. Instead of emulating Gerrard as a buccaneering no. 8 he dropped back to become the midfield anchor, still with the Herculean energy and drive but now shielding the back four, stitching together the lines between defence and attack. He didn't score as much, though when he did he celebrated as though it were his first. Klopp and Henderson might have been made for one another. As the latter told Jonathan Liew of the *Guardian*, 'When the gaffer came, I changed from wanting to be the player I thought I was – in terms of doing everything – to focusing on what the team needed.' The selflessness is typical, and how rigorously does he maintain his own and the manager's standards.* His busy shepherding and constant chivvying – it's 'One Man and His Team' – have been the beating heart of this title season.

He was there, of course, to lift the trophy itself on the night of 22 July, when we romped home 5–3 winners against Chelsea. He didn't play, ruled out of the final few games by a knee injury. The stats, which mean everything

---

* There is a very touching clip of Henderson, just named Football Writers' Association Footballer of the Year, listening in tears to a tribute online from Klopp: 'Everybody saw what a great player you are, what a great personality you have . . . I know the human being behind the player would deserve an award as well.'

and nothing, inform us that in 2019–20 LFC dropped more points (eight) in the eight games Henderson missed than in the 30 games he featured in (seven). The inevitable lapse in intensity once we were over the line had been seized upon by City, who beat us 4–0 at the Etihad. Klopp was noticeably tetchy in the post-match interview with Geoff Shreeves, partly due to the latter's slightly imbecilic line of questioning but mostly, one suspects, because of the players' failure to match the Olympian standards they had set themselves. There was another blip at the Emirates when slips by Virgil and Alisson – collector's items, both – gifted Arsenal an annoying 2–1 win. That loss also meant we wouldn't be overhauling City's 100-point record in the PL, but honestly – who cared?

The ceremony, conducted on a newly erected platform on the Kop, was a strange spectacle. Anfield, bathed in red lights, and all but empty, did its best to create a sense of triumph with fireworks and lights and Kenny Dalglish on the podium handing out the medals to the players. Klopp, applauding from the wings with his staff, wore a baseball cap reversed, like an American jock's – maybe my least favourite headgear ever – but he looked ecstatic, and I loved him for that.

A few days later Klopp was named the League Managers' Association Manager of the Year. It came with a video message of good wishes from Alex Ferguson, the man chiefly responsible for consigning Liverpool to a three-decade wait for a league title. He congratulated

'Jürgen' on his win ('Your personality runs right throughout the whole club') and forgave him for ringing him up
at 3.30 in the morning to tell him that Liverpool had won
the league. Klopp graciously returned the compliment in a
video message of his own: '[Sir Alex] was the first British
manager I met. We had breakfast together. It was long ago
and I am not sure he remembers, but I remember it forever
because, in this moment, it was like meeting the Pope.'

An arch rival – the one-time manager of Man Utd, no
less – pays sincere homage to the manager of LFC for
his first title win. Somewhere, I think, the ghost of Bill
Shankly is smiling.

10. Klopp Forever

Footballers may count it both a blessing and a burden that they are idolised. Who wouldn't enjoy the adulation for a job most of them love doing and are paid handsomely for? On the other hand, who could bear the pious reminders from management and media that you're also a 'role model'? You become a professional footballer because you have talent, ambition, opportunity: if you're lucky, and tenacious, you can make a good living out of it. But you don't become one thinking, 'Yesss! Now I can make a difference in society by setting an example to youngsters everywhere.'

Once you're in the public eye, however, your behaviour is held to account simply because you're watched by people – young impressionable males – who will follow your lead. It's odd. Nobody thinks of film stars or the spoilt princelings of pop as role models – quite the reverse – and yet they are as closely monitored as top-flight footballers.

This onus of responsibility devolves on football because it fits as a crucible of moral character. Because of the money they earn players are expected to 'give back' to the community, such as supporting charities or making hospital visits. If they appear to drag their feet there will be a health minister calling them out as ingrates. Most of them do it with good grace, and during the pandemic certain principled players like Marcus Rashford, Wilf Zaha and Jordan Henderson have gone beyond the call of duty to raise money for the indigent and helpless. In June Rashford actually effected a U-turn in government policy over food vouchers for low-income households. It may be cause for dismay that a 22-year-old footballer can show a keener moral authority than the prime minister and his cabinet.

What also sets footballers apart in the role-model stakes is their week-by-week visibility; there is no hiding from the crowd or the cameras scrutinising your every move on matchday. Diving, play-acting, the 'professional foul' (was ever a cynical foul more cynically named?), none of these things look great close up. I used to watch games with friends of an older generation who objected to the sight of players spitting – a habit so pervasive it almost goes unnoticed, though in the age of coronavirus that might change. And that's just the reflexive spitting to clear the sinuses. Spitting *at* someone is guaranteed to get people in a right old lather of indignation. To listen to Alan Shearer wax wrathful about it you'd think it was on a par with garrotting someone. I'm not sure the offence is any worse than a career-threatening tackle or mobbing a referee like a pack of hyenas, *à la* that infamous Fergie-era photograph of Roy Keane and other United players getting in the face of Andy D'Urso.

In terms of temperament football provides an interesting spiritual thermometer. To put it another way, the game finds you out. This is true at all levels, even the very lowest, where I play. Only on the football field have I observed the Jekyll-and-Hyde duality of the sporty British male. Only there will you find your mild-mannered teammate suddenly dropping the mask and snarling in someone's face that they're a 'c**t'. Usually, extreme behaviour on the astroturf stays there, and you resume your civilised interaction over a coffee afterwards. But sometimes a genuine rift is born. I lost a friend some years ago after the slow but inexorable revelation of another personality – angry, solipsistic – brooding behind his public front. Its emergence was first precipitated by our weekly game of five-a-side, and I wasn't the only one who noticed it. His example, and that of another regular, prompted me to write a short story, 'Team Player', about the desperate and comical nature of male competitiveness.* A handful of footie friends read it and straightaway recognised the characters' real-life counterparts. But one of them surprised me by saying, 'It's about all of us, really, isn't it?'

Was it? I began to wonder. Most of us lose our temper now and again, maybe give way to a volley of verbals, but on the whole I considered myself, in the words of Henry Higgins, 'a most forgiving man'. It just wasn't my style to get in someone's face. Or so I thought.

I once had a 'Zidane moment' that left the people who saw it with jaws on the floor. It was not, alas, a sensational left-footed volley that flew into the top corner. This was

---

* You can read it here at https://unbound.com/boundless/2019/09/24/team-player-by-anthony-quinn

something that required no skill at all, and revealed a volatility I had never suspected myself capable of.

January 17th: What a day this was – a horrible surprise for me and for others. Friday footie, as per, a good game in which we were leading. I'd been fouled a couple of times by O., niggly ones (his speciality) and just before half-time I gave him a tap on his ankles and we squared up. Suddenly I had his big meaty face in front of me, and in a moment of rage I just nutted him, quite hard. I recall now the shock on his face – there was a tiny delay before he realised what I'd done. I regretted it instantly. I think I regretted it almost as I was doing it, but I couldn't stop myself. Someone grabbed hold of me and sort of jounced me to the edge of the pitch, calling me a 'f—ing maniac'. The game stopped in its tracks, and I began to walk as J. [the referee] established what had just happened. I walked back and apologised to O., who was decent enough to shake hands. Down in the dressing room I suddenly felt very low indeed . . . Walked home in a daze, slipping from disbelief to self-rebuke to shame, like beads on a rosary, never-ending. To have nutted someone! Something I've never done in my life before. What had possessed me?

I began this story 'I once had . . .' as though to suggest it was a disgraceful episode of my youth. Actually, it was *this year.* January 17th, 2020. You'd think as a middle-aged man I'd know better than to assault someone on a football field. But you live and learn. The news was soon humming around the players' grapevine, and I received some kind-hearted messages of support, undeserving though I was. One came from our shocked gaffer, who hadn't been there, asking if everything was OK. I think he was rather annoyed to have missed it. The remorse, which had been instant and extreme, hung around. There was shame, too, in being the first player in our game guilty of 'violent conduct'. No one else, not even my angry estranged friend, had ever stooped to that. And having been sent off – also a first – I had to serve a four-week suspension. Banned! When the first empty Friday morning came round I felt strangely delinquent. (Was I banned from *all* football, I wondered, or could I go to our local park and find a game?) I also had to put up with my wife's joshing, pretending to cower around me now that she knew my latent propensity for violence.

I deserved it all – the jokes, the pity, the ban. Humiliating to be taught a lesson for something I'd considered beneath me. Hereafter I would not be so quick to condemn. I would never write another story about bad behaviour on the field. And I would endeavour (so help me God) not to make such an arse of myself again. My rehabilitation was interrupted by the coronavirus and the wholesale mothballing of football. Maybe by the time our five-a-side game resumes my fall from grace will have been forgotten. But I'm not banking on it.

*

The only reason I can bear to recount this is something I read afterwards about Klopp. His passionate theatrics on the touchline are so well known as to be almost a 'trademark', and have got him into trouble. He speaks quite proudly of his first red card as a coach: 'I approached the fourth official and said, "How many mistakes are allowed here? If it's fifteen you have one more."' As an example of dissent that actually qualifies as wit. He nevertheless demands discipline of his players. The hugs and laughs he shares with them in public are only one aspect of a relationship that involves respect and trust. 'He's your friend but he's not your best friend,' said Dejan Lovren, significantly. Klopp looks easy-going but he's a stickler for loyalty, as the example of Mamadou Sakho revealed. On a team tour of the US Sakho was sent home after repeated infractions and then went on social media to moan about being sidelined: his final mistake. He was dropped from the first-team squad and later moved on to Crystal Palace.

As a player himself 'Kloppo' was known to be impulsive, shouty, as often a goad to his teammates as to his opponents. He would get on people's nerves. In his 2016 biography of Klopp Elmar Neveling relates the extraordinary story of Klopp being hooked up to a lie detector for an interview with *RUND* football magazine. Asked about his worst meltdown he confessed to having headbutted his friend and Mainz teammate Sandro Schwarz: 'He'd put me on the floor twice in training. I got up, all I could see was his face in front of me, and then he was down on the ground. I wanted to die, I just wanted to die, I couldn't bear the thought of what I'd done.'

You cannot imagine the relief I felt on reading that. I was not alone in my infamy. Even Homer nods. Or nuts.

The most important of the least important things. Football is, or should be, a great distraction, an engrossing side-show, a fabulous escape from life. But it's not a substitute for life. Shankly's famous line wrote itself into the book of immortal quotations; too bad he was wrong. If your life is only football then you're not living it properly, and you're probably not doing football any favours either. I think Klopp understands this, that we walk the earth for more meaningful reasons – human connection, the possibility of making a difference, the happiness of love and knowledge and adventure. In his TV interview with Jana Schäfer he took a self-deprecating line when considering his career: 'I know a little bit more about football than some people, that's true, but it doesn't make me a special person. Five hundred years ago I would have slept in the street. I'm really lucky that my best skill somehow is needed out there.' Typically, he speculated again on what his usefulness might have been in an age without football. 'Five hundred years ago I could have danced in front of the king probably, that's it. Then I'd be back sleeping in the street.' In fact we got a glimpse of Klopp's dancing via mobile footage of the wild celebrations in Formby on title night. On the evidence of his terpsichorean talent I'd guess the Klopp of 1520 would have spent more time in the street than at court. You can't be great at everything.

The Australian historian Greg Dening once wrote, 'Nothing is so fleeting as sporting achievement, and nothing so lasting as the recollection of it.' I console myself with this wise reflection. Our capacity for sharing memories of footballing greatness is in some way more valuable than the trophies that greatness has earned. Mourinho can put three fingers up in a press room whenever he feels disrespected – i.e. most of the time – but is his style of dogged anti-football cherished in the collective memory?

This question recurs to me: Would you rather LFC had won a title with any manager between 2015 and 2019, or would you rather have won nothing with Klopp? I can say, in all honesty, I'd take the latter every time. Because what matters isn't just *that* you win, but *how* you win, and with whom. When Klopp arrived at Liverpool in 2015 his stock was sky-high from the wonders he'd performed at Dortmund. The club he was joining, conversely, had been on a downward spiral after years – decades – of underachievement. The risk to reputation was all on his side. It took Klopp nearly (only) five years to get us to the top, yet I wouldn't count the time as anything other than a blast, for alongside Man City we came to play the most exhilarating brand of football in Premier League history, under a coach who's the envy of world football.

His assistant Pep Lijnders calls him 'a true leader', adding, 'There is a saying that people don't care how much you know until they know how much you care. And I think everyone who works with Jürgen has the feeling he really cares about you and your development.'

At present there is an alarming scarcity in British life of public figures we revere or admire. Or even like. I can think of very few in politics or the media or business whose example young people might be encouraged to emulate. There is a poverty of inspiration out there. All the more reason why in this era of dire tumult and anxiety we look to someone who has not just authority but common sense, decency, a will to honour the life we have been given, and the wit to enjoy it. Jürgen Klopp isn't just for Liverpool. He isn't just for his adoring fans and the quote-hungry sports media either. He is for all of us.

Acknowledgements

I would like to thank Angus Cargill, Jon Wood, Peter Straus, Markus Naegele, Paul Baillie-Lane, Ian Critchley. I have been immeasurably encouraged in writing this book by my brothers, Mike and Pete, and by my sister, Sarah. Rachel Cooke was as ever my first and best reader, and with good grace has endured my obsession with – no, call it by its real name – love of Jürgen Klopp.

I read two very enjoyable biographies, *Klopp: Bring the Noise* (2017) by Raphael Honigstein and *Jürgen Klopp: The Biography* (2019) by Elmar Neveling. I also found useful *Shankly* (1976) by Bill Shankly and *Shanks: The Authorised Biography of Bill Shankly* (1996) by Dave Bowler ('Foreword by Mrs Shankly'). *McIlvanney on Football* (1994) by Hugh McIlvanney was never far from my reach. I have a mini-library of books about Liverpool, so let me name just one – *Liverpool, Wondrous Place* (2002) by Paul Du Noyer, a valentine to the city's music and a valuable para-history besides.

I am indebted to a number of websites, including guardian.com, times.co.uk, bbc.co.uk, youtube.com, lfchistory.net, thisisanfield.com, liverpoolfc.com, liverpoolecho.co.uk, theanfieldwrap.com, theathletic.com.